$04.95

D0076220

THE
GOOFICON

a repair manual for English

THE
GOOFICON

a repair manual for English

MARINA K. BURT

Language Director
Bilingual Planning and Research Center
Cambridge, Massachusetts

CAROL KIPARSKY

Teacher of English as a
Second Language

Newbury House Publishers

NEWBURY HOUSE PUBLISHERS, INC.

Language Science
Language Teaching
Language Learning

68 Middle Road, Rowley, Massachusetts 01969

*Copyright © 1972 by Newbury House Publishers, Inc.
All rights reserved. No part of this publication may be
reproduced without prior written permission from the
publishers.*

LIBRARY OF CONGRESS CATALOGUE No.: 78-120807
ISBN: 912066-07-5

First printing: September, 1972
Second printing: March, 1974
Third printing: April, 1975

Printed in the U.S.A.

To Heidi, Paul, and Michael

ACKNOWLEDGEMENTS

We would like to thank Phyllis Hershfang, Haj Ross, Alex Lipson, Heidi Dulay, Paul Kiparsky, John Schumann, and Joe Maffig, who provided invaluable comments on earlier versions of this work. The first draft of this work was sponsored by Language Research Foundation.

Marina K. Burt
Carol Kiparsky

ACKNOWLEDGMENTS

TABLE OF CONTENTS

†Was a riot last night.
†Is one oil company in Mexico.
†Are too many people here.
†Is raining.
†Is nice that you are here.

†John tall.
†My sisters very pretty.
†My brother a good doctor.
†He not here. No one here.
†We too big for the pony.

†I bought in Japan.
†Donald is mean so no one likes.
†Everyone wants.
†At Joey's house yesterday we really enjoyed.

†I need an I-20 form. Please send me as soon as
  possible.
†Do you like this dress? I made myself.
†I'm hungry. Please give a pretzel.

†My father been so fortunate. Hold a big post in the
  government.
†My mother been the first wife of our father. Always
  lead the other wives wherever they are invited.
†Abdul not enjoyed the party. Went home early.

†Because cannot enter in your course in January, I
  decide to apply for the fall term.
†My friend said that if not take this bus, we are late for
  school.
†I am waiting until find rich man.
†He worked until fell over.

†Escaped the professor from prison.
†Walked the priest very far.
†Was falling a lot of rain.
†Slept Rip Van Winkle twenty years.

†English use many countries.
†Girl Pramilla biting doggie.
†Much money will get a politician.
†An active president has chosen our country.

CHAPTER 2 THE AUXILIARY SYSTEM

†Do I must take an entrance exam?
†Why don't you can send two pounds?
†Does she have come yet?
†Does he be going?
†Never do you must spit like that.
†Nowhere do you can see so many people.
†I don't have gone yet.
†He doesn't be studying tonight.

†Why we bow to each other?
†How Americans dress themselves?

†Paints the boy?
†Go you to school?
†When began the game?
†There lives your teacher?

†I did leave yesterday.
†He does spend his holidays always at Benin.
†We do go to church every Sunday.
†Our priest did give each one a cushion.

†I practice not religion.
†He writes not good books.
†He saw not the beautiful lady.

†The horse not eats the meat.
†Not run here.
†I not went yesterday.

†Why did he went?
†Does she likes it here?
†You didn't sent the form.
†Not only did I ate too much.
†I did not spent too much money.

†He must written it.

†I can to go.
†I should to read English all the time.

†You have could do it if you wanted to.
†No one is may leaving now.

†I must can catch this train.
†You must will send me money.
†We shall can leave tomorrow, isn't it?
†I should must going tomorrow.

†She has been smoking less, isn't it?
†He won't come tonight, is it?
†You like French brandy, isn't it?

CHAPTER 3   PASSIVE SENTENCES

†The bread finished.
†Each cushion given by our priest.
†I have impressed greatly with the ideas of Plato.
†They have invited and they came.
†I have so disappointed with you.
†The hymn was singing so beautiful.

†There were many things which were practicing, such as thuggery, bribery and disturbance.

CHAPTER 4   TEMPORAL CONJUNCTIONS

†After to study, you must visit your father.
†Since that saw it, he is very sorry.

†John sleeps a lot after eats a lot.

†Since that he has seen her, he has been cheerful.
†After that we walked, we felt very warm.
†He married Ketcha after that he got rich.
†Let's go to see him while that he is here.

†He got rich until he married.
†I lost my wallet until Juan gave it back.
†He put on his clean shirt after he wanted to go.
†After Robert kept his coat on the hook, he sat down
to eat.

†Since the child recovered from measles, he grew well.
†He died until the doctor came.
†They learned French until their tutor quit.
†The ball crashed through the window while she knitted
a sock nearby.

†They were telling us a hundred times.
†She kept her patience while the baby was repeatedly
dropping his spoon.
†We listened while the teacher was pronouncing the
word again and again.

†I did it while they didn't look.
†You should practice on your drum while he doesn't study.

†After he didn't come, we went looking for him.
†We had to water the garden after it hadn't rained
recently.

†No one should say bad things about him while he is
dead.
†Life is complicated while you are old.
†We picked these oranges while they were rotten.
†My nephew was grown up while he was in college.

†The fruit had become rotten until we could eat it.
†Everything was eaten up until we came.

4.6 Superficial tense agreement (STAGR)

4.6.1 Failure to apply STAGR with BEFORE, AFTER, UNTIL, WHILE, WHEN

†He was rich until he marries.
†I don't have any money until he gave me some.
†He wrote the letter after he has found the address.
†After John drinks the wine, he was sick.

†When you were here yesterday, you have promised to send your picture.
†After our last pennies have been spent, we wanted to continue our way to Begemdir.
†My father has lived in Begemdir until he died.
†The people in the top posts in this world worked until they have reached at their different posts.

4.6.2 Inconsistency in perfect use: WHILE

†While you have worked, I make phone calls.
†While he has been playing, I am doing all the work.
†She has been making tea while you are sleeping.

4.6.3 STAGR misapplied: SINCE

†I am glad since I came to this country.
†They are studying in this school since they are six years old.
†I am studying English since I am six but I cannot speak it.
†Since we left in the morning we only had a liquid food.
†Since he won the lottery, he is happy.

4.7 Superfluous WILL and other future constructions

†We will eat after we will pray.
†Before you will leave, you will kiss Grandma.
†I am going to leave here when the new supervisor is going to come.
†We will not eat while he will be standing up.

PEDAGOGICAL NOTES

CHAPTER 5 SENTENTIAL COMPLEMENTS

†The neighbors say both children he teases.
†He says that he no money has.
†Rufus hopes that is going to U.S.A. soon.
†It is too bad that he coming now.

†It is too late milk to buy.
†They are interested in horses riding.
†I want you to see married.
†You will just love Weeki Wachi. I want you to take there.

†Surprises me that he wears a wig.
†Is very hard for me to learn English right.
†Was too bad that the priest could not come.

†That is funny to see him today.
†That is strange to meet your cousin here.
†He astonishes me that America is so big.
†He is raining today.
†He is warm in here!

†It was a very tall man here for you.
†It have a dog in here.
†It will be some club meetings on Tuesday.

†There is the library key here.
†There looked a strange man through the window.
†There are some elephants very ferocious.

†I couldn't walk yet after the baby was born, so the doctor didn't want to go home.
†Daddy has a lot of work. Mother expects to stay at his office late.

†I couldn't sleep until you got back. It worries me to stay out so late.
†It astonishes me to be here; I thought you were in London.

†I think to have my I.D. card here.
†Anna told the priest to have six children.

†Him to be so rich is unfair.
†We plan our class to take a trip.
†I am sorry for him be disappointed.

†No one regrets them going away.
†He voting that way was terrible.
†For me failing the exam would make Mother upset.

†It is necessary for finish the work.
†It is impossible for to leave right now.
†I will try for drive faster.
†For to catch the bus, go to the next corner.

†Why won't you let me to go?
†You must have Cielo to bake some delicious bread.

†Taxes make people to be miserable.
†The doctor can't make her to be thin.
†I just can't make the car to be pretty any more.

†The vacuum cleaner makes easy to clean the house.
†They found pleasant to see you.

†He is unusual to have a new auto.
†Volkswagen buses are impossible to go too fast.
†The door is strange to be unlocked.

†A girl was decided to play the piano.
†We were demanded to return the hymn book.

†We plan on finish this today.
†My mother believes in to say grace before to eat.
†I laughed at to hear it.
†I was delighted at him to resign.

†I am used to go without breakfast.
†His behavior will lead to go to prison.
†We look forward to see you again.

†I prevented him to going with me.
†We kept him for to see her.

†I cannot prevent you from to do that, but I'm not responsible.
†You must not discourage him from to write what he must.
†Why do you prohibit your sister from to kiss me?

†Mark thinks the beans needing fertilizer.
†He resented that I went.
†We will want that he visits us.

†Why did you tell them not looking at each other?
†Nobody wants doing that.
†I don't expect seeing him today.
†We will offer carrying the furniture.
†Remember putting out the trash tomorrow.

†I resent Tom to come home so late.
†Don't you remember to see her yesterday?
†Most of the pupils enjoy to have a holiday.
†Let's ignore him to bother us.

†I will enjoy to swim.
†They had hoped going, but couldn't.

CHAPTER 6   PSYCHOLOGICAL PREDICATES

†The cat is on the dinner table, but my father doesn't
  bother that.
†I have impressed Plato.
†Do you surprise me?
†Call your mother; she worries you.

†And physical geography prefer me more than anything
  else.
†The party enjoyed Aziz.
†Do I love you? Tell me yes.

†I surprise that he likes it.
†I delight that you are so thin.
†His parents annoy that he always goes to the cinema.

†We were all bored about his teaching.

†I was surprising that he came.
†I was boring with his speech.
†Tell me what you are disgusting by.
†He is so interesting in business.

†Don't go to that movie. It bores.
†When Judge Fielding takes his cloak off, he doesn't
  impress very much.
†When Americans excite, they talk too fast for me.
†Why did you depress yesterday?

INTRODUCTION

Goof: *(goof)* slang. n. 1. an error students tend to make in learning English as a second language, for which no blame is implied. 2. a sentence containing one or more goofs.

Gooficon: *(goof'i kon)* slang. n. a collection of goofs and their explanations from the point of view of English grammar.

The Gooficon has been prepared to help both experienced and inexperienced teachers of English as a second language whose students already know some English but still make mistakes.

We have collected many kinds of goofs that students from various languages seem to make regularly. We group them into various areas of syntax and then discuss the grammar which is pertinent to the goofs actually made. The areas of grammar in which foreign students have difficulty seem to be quite general, although the particular mistakes made in some areas vary. We hope that the linguistic insights we have found to be helpful in pinpointing many kinds of mistakes will be of use to other ESL (English as a Second Language) teachers.

Selection of Data

The data in *The Gooficon* is based on many sentences collected from spoken and written learners' English originating all over the world. They include our own observations and those of other teachers, including Peace Corps Volunteers. The examples are not always "raw." Often they have been simplified by partial repairing to display the goof under discussion more clearly. Simplifying the sentences produced by students is not a subterfuge. It is useful to isolate a goof. Often a sentence heard in the classroom sounds very strange, but there is so much wrong with it that it is hard to pick out any single problem. Hopefully if a teacher has seen some goof in isolation, and has studied the relevant grammar, he is more apt to be able to pick it out of the garble. Goofs, whether verbatim or simplified, are

1

preceded by a dagger (†).[1]

Part of the function of the analysis is to focus on and explain mistakes which are not simple to locate, let alone correct and explain. We have not spent too much time on mistakes whose sources are obvious, such as subject-verb agreement, singular and plural formation, tenses which are misformed, etc. These mistakes are the ones most often recognized and corrected by most ESL teachers already. But many other kinds of goofs require a deeper knowledge of the grammar of English to understand and explain.

Of course, not every perplexing error teachers can expect to hear has been covered, but only a selection of typical ones. Another criterion for the goofs included in this book is the relative ease with which their sources and corrections can be explained. Prepositions and idioms, for example, are not handled because we know of no set rules that will be of general help. Pronunciation is also excluded here.

Purpose and organization

We intend this book to be used not as a substitute for other ESL materials, but to help teachers make decisions about how best to use their materials to suit the particular problems and needs of their students.

The chapters are arranged on the basis of groups of errors that fall together structurally. Each chapter or section opens with examples of the types of errors to be analyzed and discussed there. Any definitions which are essential to the subsequent chapter are also given.

The *Analysis of Goof Types* includes statements of those rules of English structure which the student will have to control in order to overcome the goofs. (This does not necessarily mean that the students are expected to learn the rules as such.) The purpose of this section is to clarify for the teacher what, grammatically, is behind the errors his student

---

[1]Some verbatim goofs, once their major faults are corrected, will still display minor errors which we assume the teacher will recognize and deal with as he feels necessary.

It is common practice for transformational grammarians to prefix any ungrammatical sequence of words with an asterisk (*). These can include sentences that no one would say. Since we are only interested in sentences actually spoken or written by people learning ESL, we will draw the distinction by prefixing spoken ungrammatical sentences (uncorrected goofs) with the dagger †.

makes. The section does not present ready-to-teach materials, or specify in what order to teach the subject matter. The order in which particular goofs are discussed in the chapter is determined by simplicity of exposition: simpler mistakes are discussed before more complex ones. If the reader should find himself teaching a course in English grammar, this section of each chapter could provide the skeleton of the course. But for usual pedagogical purposes, most of this material would not be made explicit in this way in class.

Each chapter concludes with a section of *Pedagogical Notes*. This section includes a summary of those points or rules of thumb that might be used directly in class. There are practical suggestions for devices that will be effective in making the point to the student and recommendations of practice materials, drills, etc., which will be most useful for getting students to remember and use them. These ideas on how to help students overcome difficulties are not all-inclusive, but may suggest fruitful types of practice which the teacher can adapt to his students' needs. In addition, we often discuss the relative importance of the goofs for comprehension and communication, and where possible make recommendations as to their order of correction.

Learning the student's "error regularities"

One aim of *The Gooficon* is to help the teacher handle a role which is seldom explicitly treated, and for which present materials are not appropriate: to recognize and respond to the particular problems of his own students by becoming thoroughly familiar with their error regularities. We stress that we do not mean this in the sense of contrastive analysis with respect to syntax, for we have not found that the majority of syntactical goofs are due to the native language syntax of the learner.

Because we have not found "foreign syntax" to be a major factor in describing learner goofs, *The Gooficon* is not language specific. Instead, it simply displays some parts of English grammar which cause speakers of many different native languages difficulty. After listening to student speech, the teacher will become prepared to determine what fact of English grammar the students must learn.

For example, suppose a student makes this goof:

†That car driven by a mad man.

It is not always enough just to tell him to add an *is* or *was* right after *car* and leave it at that. What about *be* in the rest of his speech? Does he in general skip *be?* Does he also say things like these:

> †He tall.
> †She a nurse.

Or does he have trouble only with the auxiliary *be?*

> †He running too fast.
> †He not singing now.

He may have a general problem with *be*, or he may have to learn to use it just with passives or just with progressives. The teacher who knows his student's general speech will be able to determine what rule of English the student needs to learn in order to correct a particular type of goof.

The need to decide which goofs to correct

The most concrete situation where such dialect knowledge is essential is when students are talking freely. It is quite common for a conscientious teacher to try to give the student a perfect sentence with all the errors removed in place of the student's imperfect one.

However, correcting every goof has come drawbacks. The student gets no chance to say any more and often loses his train of thought. And frequently he has difficulty relating the shiny new sentence or paragraph to what he was trying to say.

We suggest another strategy instead:

1. Listen to what the student is saying for a while.
2. Select a manageable number of important goofs.
3. Work consistently on those until there is some improvement.

To work on a goof can mean to:

- simply correct it whenever it comes up,
- teach a lesson about the point, or
- reinforce the point by drills.

For written work, we suggest correcting important goofs in one color, and all the others in black. Then the student can focus on a few things at a time. After these have been fixed, he can begin working on less important goofs.

Using the hierarchy

To help the teacher choose which goofs to correct, we offer suggestions on their place in the hierarchy. This is a way of ordering goofs according to their importance. The worst mistakes are those that interfere most with comprehension and communication, while unimportant mistakes do not greatly interfere with communication. We recommend working on goofs in order of importance wherever possible.

To see what we mean by hierarchy, look at any sentence or paragraph riddled with goofs. Then try correcting one at a time, keeping the rest uncorrected. From this procedure, you can easily see which goofs make the most difference to the comprehensibility of the whole sentence.

For example, if your students say things like this, what should be corrected first?

†English language use much people.

There are three goofs:

1. *The* is missing before *English language*.
2. The *much/many* distinction is not observed.
3. Word order in the whole sentence is wrong.

Let's correct them one at a time:

1. The English language use much people.	the *inserted*
2. English language use many people.	much *corrected*
3. Much people use English language.	*word order corrected*

It would be widely agreed that the third rendition is the most comprehensible and gets the message across best.

From the above discussion, we can say that word order outweighs correct noun phrase formation. The word order is more important than either the *much/many* distinction in the noun phrase *many people* or the presence of an article in *the English language*.

It might at first glance seem better to make a passive out of the original example, since that doesn't change the student's original sentence as drastically. That is, correct the sentence to:

> English language is used by much people.

However, we suggest that before doing that, you first consider whether basic word order is a general problem in the student's dialect. If it is, it should be chased down at every opportunity, as it is clearly one of the most important things for him to get straight in order to be generally understood. Wherever alternative corrections to a goof are possible, your assessment of the student's general skill and his characteristic problems can guide you in deciding which one to teach.

There is another consideration in ordering corrections: generality of the rule violated. For instance, there may be something that makes utter mincemeat of a sentence, but which is unlikely to affect other sentences very often. A rarely used idiom might be said completely wrong so that the entire sentence sounds incomprehensible. However, it may often be better to correct something less devastating in that particular sentence, something that has more general application in English, such as word order, or question formation.

Global and local goofs

In sentences with more than one clause, mistakes in overall organization which confuse the relations among the constituent clauses, such as which precedes which, outweigh minor goofs in any one clause. Overall goofs are called "global," and minor goofs within clauses are called "local." For example:

Clause 1	*Clause 2*

†Since the harvest was good, was rain a lot last year.

The mistakes are these:

Since is attached to the wrong clause.	*global*
Subject *it* is missing.	*local*
Form of verb *was rain* should be *rained*.	*local*

The goofs in Clause 2 are local because they are confined to a single clause. But misplacing the conjunction *since* is a global mistake, as it affects both clauses. *Since*, like all conjunctions, relates the two clauses: it tells which came first.

Now let's first correct the local mistakes, leaving *since* alone:

> Since the harvest was good, it rained a lot last year.   *local goofs*
> *corrected*

Next, we'll correct only the placement of the conjunction, leaving the local goofs alone:

> The harvest was good since was rain a lot last year.   *global goof*
> *corrected*

We can see that correcting the placement of *since* adds the most to the sentence meaning as a whole.

From the examples above, we see that any one correction improves the sentence, but some do much more for the sentence than others. A by-product of the hierarchy is the notion of correcting one goof at a time. This does not mean teachers have to utter goofs themselves, but rather to *tolerate* some goofs while others are being worked on by the students.

This may sound quite different from the usual teaching theory about allowing only correct speech in the classroom, or at least demanding it as much as possible. But we feel that just as a mother or father does not force a child to speak adult English from the start, for the obvious reason that the child is unable to do it anyway, so second language learners, adults included, should be given the same opportunity to practice and improve to the extent that they are able. It is useless and unnecessarily painful to attempt too much at once.

Although we are assuming generally that global mistakes interfere with comprehension much more than local mistakes, there are some local mistakes that also interfere a great deal with comprehension. These should be corrected early. For example, students may mix up accusative and possessive pronouns:

> †Please send my as soon as possible the book I want.

Case marking is a local mistake, but with a pronoun it is important to get it right, since case marking makes clear the grammatical relations in the sentence.

Another important local mistake is confusing *which* with *that*:

†I know which you left early.

This is hard to make sense of, unless you happen to know the student's own language has only one word for both *which* (relative pronoun) and *that* (conjunction).

Closely related goofs

Another consideration is how closely certain goofs are related to each other. Sometimes it is better to correct pairs of mistakes. For example:

† I just saw Abdul, but I think *not here now.*

In the italicized clause (or part of one), two things are missing: the nominative subject, *he*, and the form of the verb *be* which should follow it. In these cases, it seems more helpful to tell the student to put in both the nominative subject and a verb (*is*) to agree with it, since he must not use one without the other. Having a nominative subject and an agreeing verb is what makes a finite clause, a notion which is very general and important for the student to learn.

A similar mistake is to have the subject missing and its position followed by a tenseless verb:

†I think *leaving* now.

In the italicized portion, a nominative subject is missing, and the verb form *leaving* would not be right even if the subject were present, since it does not agree with any subject in English.

†I think
$$\begin{matrix} \text{I} \\ \text{we} \\ \text{he} \\ \text{you} \end{matrix}$$
leaving now.

Since presence of a nominative subject means the following verb must agree with it, the two goofs should be corrected together.

Provision of rules

We have tried to organize the goofs according to what the person who says them has to learn about English, such as *word order, the passive construction,* or *sentence comple-ment types.* Our way of expressing what a person has to learn is frequently in the form of a rule which he has been violat-ing. Whether students should learn these rules explicitly or implicitly is up to the teacher. It will depend on student needs.

Obviously, a book like this cannot be too technical, or it will not be helpful. We have included only the linguistic analysis that has been useful to us in our past experience. This kind of analysis often makes clear just what it is the student does not know about the grammar, or what rule he must learn to avoid a particular goof. For example, consider the following goofs:

†Do I must go?
†Why do you are leaving so soon?
†I don't can speak English.

Only one rule has not been learned:

> *Do* never appears in the same clause with an auxiliary.

Simple rules like this are easy to pass on to students, and in our book, they are put in boxes for easy reference. But all the rules we give are as simple as this. The more involved rules are primarily for the benefit of the teacher, so that he is better able to diagnose and decide how to treat student problems.

When we state a rule, we will often call it a "white lie." This means that if the rule is followed, the student will not be wrong, even though he may hear correct sentences where our rule was not followed. For example, one white lie is that:

> Pronouns are not dropped in English.

Even though he may hear *Dave got tired and went home,* if he says *Dave got tired and he went home,* he won't be wrong. Rules will also be in dashed boxes when they express a partial truth. A trustworthy rule will be boxed in solid lines:

> To form negatives, put *not* after the first aux-iliary.

Linguistic terminology

We often talk about rules like this:

> To form questions, put the question word first, if there is one, and place the first auxiliary in front of the subject.

This kind of talk presupposes that there is a more basic sentence with a first auxiliary in some other place. In other words, one sentence is changed into another when a question is formed. We consider grammar rules as a way of deriving, or making, sentences from other sentences. So, we say that the question is derived by the above rule from the corresponding declarative sentence:

He can make it. Can he make it?

Sometimes we need more than just the words present to relate sentences to each other. For example, how do we relate these?

He came. Did he come?

Sentences with *do* are derived from sentences which do not originally have *do*. We will come to this in Chapter 2, Section 2.1.2, page 25.

When we talk about sentences that have a subordinate clause in them, i.e. complex sentences, we may use simple diagrams to make each clause explicit. For example, in a sentence like *We know that Peg gets clothes at Keezer's.* there are two clauses: *We know (it)* and *Peg gets clothes at Keezer's.* We may diagram them for discussion in the following way (disregarding irrelevant details):

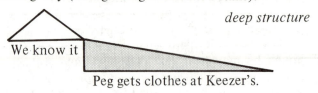

deep structure

We know it

Peg gets clothes at Keezer's.

We know that Peg gets clothes   *surface structure*
at Keezer's.

We say the second clause is "embedded" in the first, or main clause. Embedded sentences are also called subordinate constructions.

Sometimes we will show deep structures that do not look exactly like any spoken sentence. In this example, the deep structure has an *it* which does not appear in the surface structure, and *that* is inserted in the surface structure. We also separate clauses from each other to keep the grammatical relations within each clause separate, i.e., to keep clear who did what to whom in each clause. There are grammar rules that only apply to one clause at a time, and only affect one clause at a time, such as the passive rule. And some rules work so that two clauses are affected at the same time. We will discuss some of the latter in Chapters 5 and 6.

Pedagogical remarks

We often say that a student "needs to learn" some rule or other. This does not mean he should learn the rule verbatim, but that appropriate techniques should be used to get the application of that rule across. If explicit formulation helps a student, such as one who is accustomed by his education to thinking about language, to sum up what he has practiced, fine. But it is no substitute for his being able to produce and use freely the kind of correct sentences the rule generates.

When working on a goof, it is often useful to employ the common types of drills — substitution, transformation, etc. But there is nothing more deadly than to walk into class and say "Today we'll learn to ask questions in English," and proceed to form unmotivated questions for twenty minutes. Instead, we suggest starting with conversation and stopping when a student has trouble expressing a question he wants to ask. Then the class will be motivated to do a drill for a little while before turning to the conversation.

In a typical heterogenous class, one student will be able to recognize another's goof. It is very useful for students to correct each other, especially when the correcter has himself just overcome some problems. This works particularly well when answers can be right or wrong for content, not just grammar.

The Gooficon can be used in more than one way with your students. Goofs can be used to help motivate the learning of grammar by presenting them first, followed by the relevant grammar. This use can be self-instructional. Alternatively, small portions of grammar can be presented first, with goofs to be corrected following as a type of drill. This second use provides more of a presentation-and-exercise treatment.

CHAPTER 1

THE SKELETON OF ENGLISH CLAUSES

ANALYSIS OF GOOF TYPES

From grammar school, everybody knows that the *subject* of a sentence is a noun phrase which tells us what the sentence "is about." It comes first in a declarative sentence and the verb agrees in person and number with it. The predicate is the rest of the sentence. It has one indispensable part, the simple predicate. This is simply the verb itself. The verb may be followed or complemented by an object noun, or by other nouns, prepositional phrases, adverbs or clauses. The predicate "says something about" the subject of the sentence. Some goofs in this chapter such as missing subjects affect overall sentence structure and we consider them global. Others, such as wrong tense markings, are local.

1.1. Missing parts

1.1.1 Surrogate subject missing: THERE and IT

Certain subjects get left out by speakers of all sorts of languages, as varied as Spanish and Japanese:

	Missing subject
†Was a riot last night.	*there*
†Is one oil company in Mexico.	*there*
†Are too many people here.	*there*
†Is raining.	*it*
†Is nice that you are here.	*it*

Remembering to put in the subjects *there* and *it* is especially troublesome for many students. This is because the words themselves don't mean anything. We know that the above sentences are not about *there* or *it,* but about *a riot, an oil company,* etc. For one reason or another, these meaningful words come after the verb, leaving the sentence without a subject in front of the verb. The sentences are incorrect because in English:

13

> Every finite English sentence must have a subject.[1]

There and *it* are simply place holders, or surrogate subjects, to meet this demand. But they also have another use. How else would we tell if the above examples were questions or statements? As they stand, one can only tell by intonation, which is unreliable in the speech of many learners. But as soon as *there* or *it* is inserted before the verb *be*, it is clear which they are. Maybe part of the reason why English refuses to drop subjects, even vacuous ones, is because it needs them to distinguish questions and statements.

> There was a riot last night.
> Is there one oil company in Mexico?
> There are too many people here.
> Is it raining?
> It is nice that you are here.

Sometimes an observant student might ask you why people say:

> Been here long?
> Still raining outside?

Or, as a reply to *What did you do last night?* why they give an answer like:

> Went to the movies.

When he notices such informal usage, you might blush to have taught him that every English sentence must have a subject. But it is harder to learn when it is possible to leave out the subject informally than it is to learn the white lie that it must always be present. In these examples, it is just as good to have the subjects in:

> Have you been here long?
> Is it still raining outside?
> We went to the movies.

---

[1] The only place where subjects are regularly left out is imperative sentences like *Come here, Go away, Keep quiet,* etc. These are therefore not finite sentences.

The point is not to try to teach students all possible English sentences, but to teach them approximate rules or whatever else is necessary to help them avoid making goofs. If they always put a subject in a finite clause, they will not make ellipsis goofs, errors of omission. There is little reason to teach the complicated conditions under which it is permissible to omit a subject until students have firm control of basic English syntax.

1.1.2 Simple predicate missing: BE

†John tall.
†My sisters very pretty.
†My brother a good doctor.
†He not here. No one here.
†We too big for the pony.

In all of these, the simple predicate *be* has been left out. This is probably because the meaningful predicates here are the adjective or noun phrases. *Tall, very pretty, a good doctor* and *here* are the words that "tell us something about" the subject. However, these words cannot carry tense in English. Since every finite English sentence must have a tense carrier, *be* is inserted in these cases. It is just a place holder with no more meaning than *there* or *it*. These examples show:

> Every English sentence needs a verb to carry the tense.

John is tall.
My sisters are very pretty.
My brother is a good doctor.
He's not here. No one's here.
We're too big for the pony.

1.1.3 Object pronoun missing

†I bought in Japan.
†Donald is mean so no one likes.
†Everyone wants.
†At Joey's house yesterday we really enjoyed.
†I need an I-20 form. Please send me as soon as possible.
†Do you like this dress? I made myself.
†I'm hungry. Please give a pretzel.

The gap we feel in these sentences is the place where the object should be. The object (direct or indirect) in each case would be a pronoun. There are some languages which have ellipsis rules for dropping pronouns in places like this, but there is no such rule in English. Students should learn that:

> Pronouns are not dropped in English. [1]

We might consider the use of pronouns that refer back to other nouns, anaphoric pronouns, as a way English has of putting in an object where the verb requires one even though the pronoun doesn't really add anything to the meaning of the sentence. In this way, anaphoric pronouns in object positions are place holders, like *there, it,* and *be* above.

I bought it in Japan.
Donald is mean so no one likes him.
Everyone wants another.
At Joey's house yesterday we really enjoyed ourselves.
I need an I-20 form. Please send me one as soon as possible.
Do you like this dress? I made it myself.
I'm hungry. Please give me a pretzel.

1.1.4 Subject pronoun missing

Many students also omit subject pronouns when they are anaphoric.

†My father been so fortunate. Hold a big post in the government.
†My mother been the first wife of our father. Always lead the other wives wherever they are invited.
†Abdul not enjoyed the party. Went home early.

The problem with these is similar to missing anaphoric object pronouns. That is, it is pretty clear from the context what or whom the missing pronoun would refer to if it had

---

[1]This is a white lie, as pronouns can be dropped in some sentences with conjunctions. For example:
    Dave got tired and (he) went home.
and rarely:
    Harry cleaned, Heloise cooked and Arthur ate the fish.

been put in. So in many languages, this pronoun or repeated noun is simply dropped. But English does not have a pronoun-dropping rule, and so the anaphoric pronoun must be left in.

> My father been so fortunate. He hold a big post
> in the government.
> My mother been the first wife of our father.
> She always lead the other wives wherever they
> are invited.
> Abdul not enjoyed the party. He went home
> early.

For many students it is harder to learn to put in the surrogate subjects *there* and *it* than content pronouns like *he, she, they*, etc. This is probably because *there* and *it* don't mean anything, nor do they refer to anything. And some languages which don't drop pronouns like *he* and *him* still don't have meaningless pronouns like *it* or *there*.

If students leave out anaphoric subject pronouns after subordinate conjunctions; intended meanings become even more confused:

> †Because cannot enter in your course in January,
> I decide to apply for the fall term.
> †My friend said that if not take this bus, we are
> late for school.
> †I am waiting until find rich man.
> †He worked until fell over.

These goofs illustrate that the form of a clause following a subordinate conjunction must be the same as that of a main clause. Such clauses are finite, which means they must not only have finite verbs, but nominative subjects to go with them as well.

> Subordinate clauses, like main clauses, must
> have subjects and verbs.

Because I cannot enter in your course in January, I decide to apply for the fall term.
My friend said that if we not take this bus, we are late for school.
I am waiting until I find rich man.
He worked until he fell over.

1.2 Misordered parts

1.2.1 Verb before subject

In English, the subject always precede the verb in declarative sentences. However, some students say things like this:

> †Escaped the professor from prison.
> †Walked the priest very far.
> †Was falling a lot of rain.
> †Slept Rip Van Winkle twenty years.

It may be that in the student's language, it is possible or even necessary to have the verb first. Be that as it may, he must learn that:

> English word order in declarative sentences is *subject-verb-object.*

The professor escaped from prison.
The priest walked very far.
A lot of rain was falling.
Rip Van Winkle slept twenty years.

1.2.2 Subject and object permuted

Word order also causes trouble in simple clauses that have objects. Some students reverse (or permute) the positions of subject and object:

> †English use many countries.   *object-verb-subject*
> †Girl Pramilla biting doggie.
> †Much money will get a politician.
> †An active president has chosen our country.

Here one might wonder who is the doer, or agent, of the action specified by the verb. When either the subject or the object could be the agent, ambiguity arises over who did what to whom. The order of constituents, *noun-verb-noun,* is English. One could easily take the sentences at face value at first, interpreting each as if the first noun were the subject and the second the object.

> Many countries use English.   *subject-verb-object*
> Doggie biting girl Pramilla.

A politician will get much money.
Our country has chosen an active president.

The most frequent additional ordering mixups are these:

†A banana is eating the child.   *object-verb-subject*
†Is eating the child a banana.   *verb-subject-object*

Three other misorderings are logically possible, but students don't often seem to produce them:

*A banana the child is eating.   *object-subject-verb*
*The child a banana is eating.   *subject-object-verb*
*Is eating a banana the child.   *verb-object-subject*

English uses violations of the *subject-verb-object* order to put sentences in other modes. The auxiliary and subject are reordered to get questions, or the subject *you* is dropped to get the imperative. Also, an object or other noun may be placed at the beginning of a sentence for emphasis:

Chickenpox she doesn't have!

This usage, which is rather rare, might be considered an English sentence. But we cannot assume that a student whose basic word order is still shaky has such subtle intent when he produces misordered sentences.

PEDAGOGICAL NOTES

1.3 Own language distortions (OLD's)

It is easy to point out goofs in word order and ellipsis dramatically when the source of the goof is word-for-word translation from the student's own language. The technique is "own language distortions," or OLD's. The basic idea is to take the correct version of the English sentence and do a word-for-word translation into the student's own language, disregarding the syntax of his language and using that of English. The result is a very distorted sentence, a goof in his own language. For example, suppose a French student says:

†I'll him see tomorrow.

You can say to him:

† Je verrai le demain.

Or suppose a German student says:

†I know that he sick is.

You can say:

†Ich weiss dass er ist krank.

Tell him that although his language sounds funny this way, that this is how the idea is expressed in English word order, and that he sounds as strange to Americans as the distorted French or German sentence sounds to him.

This technique has several things to recommend it. First, since the vocabulary is familiar, the syntactic aspect of the sentence which is peculiar to English stands out like a sore thumb. Second, it is easy to remember as a formula, rather than trying to memorize the many new things in a sample sentence which is all English. And third, the student gets the idea that "My goof sounds funny to you the same way yours sounds funny to me."

Of course, OLD's are most effective when word order in the student's own language is rigid, as it is in English. If it is "free," or not as rigid, distortions will not have as much of an effect. In that case, it helps to strip the words of their case markings and then mix them up, since the case markings determine what relation the words have to each other in languages where word order is not so rigid.

1.4   Exercises for ellipsis

1.4.1 OLD's for ellipsis

OLD's can also be used when the goof is pronoun ellipsis by a student from a pronoun-dropping language. For example, if the language has pronouns, like Japanese, but prefers very much to drop them except in elevated speech, OLD's should insert them where they are normally dropped.

1.4.2 Tapping and humming

To help students get used to putting in pronouns, free conversation is always helpful. Almost every sentence in a conversation or narrative about someone or something needs a pronoun or two, so this is a fertile field for pointed corrections.

One way to go about correcting ellipses is to focus on the rhythm of the sentence. Simultaneously hum and tap it out, and get them into the habit of fitting their words into this pattern, so they will see they have left something out. For example, suppose a student says:

†I saw here.

The teacher can hum and tap:

Have the student first tap and hum the rhythm simultaneously himself, and then tap and fill in the words:

I saw it here.

At the earliest stage, it is progress if a student sticks anything in where the pronoun belongs, whether it's the wrong pronoun or just a hummed syllable. Once he has the idea that *some* little unstressed word belongs there after the verb, one can begin to teach him to distinguish among the pronouns.

1.4.3 Duplicate pronoun drills

A type of drill which forces students to put pronouns into sentences provides a duplicate pronoun:

Cue: Where's Harish? I saw him him in school.
Response: Where's Harish? I saw him in school.

When the students have to cross out one occurrence of *him* and leave the other it has the psychological effect of underlining the pronoun. The exercise itself is foolproof; it always comes out right since the students only have to cross out one of the repeated words. The result is automatically English. The point of this rather primitive exercise is not to make them ponder over the answer, but to make them aware of what the sentence looks and feels like. They should be encouraged to say the correct version out loud, after getting the cue either in writing or orally from the teacher or a tape.

1.5 Scrambling

A rather basic device for practicing and testing word order is scrambling. There are many ways to use this technique. For example, one can write down each major constituent of a sentence on a separate card, and ask the student to form a sentence out of those pieces:

> USE   COUNTRIES   MANY   ENGLISH

At first, another foolproof type of exercise can be used to teach them the word order in question. Put the words on cards made to interlock at the sides like a jigsaw puzzle. Solving the jigsaw puzzle automatically gives an English sentence. After a while, give the same material on simple cards, with no external cues, such as the shape of the cards, to the word order.

> VERY   WALKED   FAR   PRIEST   THE

For students who don't read easily, pictures showing the normal sequence of actions can also be used, and the words corresponding to the actions can be put underneath the pictures as captions. The student's task is then to put the picture cards in the right order, and "read" off the resulting sentence.

 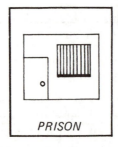 

THE PROFESSOR   PRISON   ESCAPED FROM

Scrambling has many useful applications. Another is ordering words within a large constituent such as a noun phrase:

> CLOSE   OF   FRIEND   MINE   A

In narratives, several sets of words can be presented so that each is arranged into a sentence. All of them can then be ordered into a narrative. This can be especially helpful in using anaphoric pronouns. If a student is asked to use all the cards, and if some of them are pronouns, he is forced to get used to the obligatory presence of pronouns. If ellipsis is the problem rather than word order, this is another foolproof exercise, since the pronouns provided must be used.

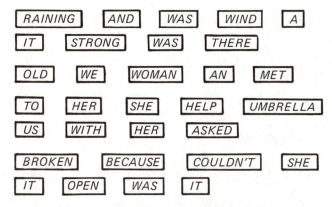

As a student becomes more independent he can be given card sets which include superfluous words. Perhaps all the prepositions and pronouns can be signalled with color as optional, meaning the student has to decide both which ones to use and where to put them.

If the problem is ellipsis of pronouns, he can be given extra pronoun cards, which may be marked as optional, and different sentences can be made.

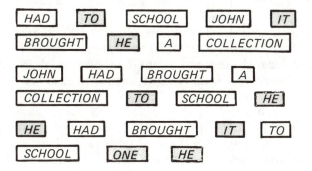

CHAPTER 2

THE AUXILIARY SYSTEM

ANALYSIS OF GOOF TYPES

2.1 The use of DO

2.1.1 Overuse in questions and negatives

†Do I must take an entrance exam?
†Why don't you can send two pounds?
†Does she have come yet?
†Does he be going?
†Never do you must spit like that.
†Nowhere do you can see so many people.
†I don't have gone yet.
†He doesn't be studying tonight.

These sentences, produced by students of various language backgrounds, are really not hard to understand, but they have a definitely un-English ring. Most auxiliary goofs are local goofs, unless word order is affected. We might correct them by drilling each one separately as it comes up in conversation, but this makes it look as though each goof is unique. This isn't true. All the sentences share one serious offender, the little word *do*.

Do never shows up with *can, could, shall, should, will, would, may, might* or *must*. The technical name for this group of nine words is modal auxiliaries or modals. We'll see that modals act as a team in other ways in English too.

But this is not all. In the last two examples there are no modals present, and *do* should not be in there either. This means that the students will have to learn about the word *do* that it does not appear in the same sentence with a modal nor with the auxiliaries *have* and *be*.[1]

---

[1]*Do* of course is used with *have* when *have* is not an auxiliary but a main verb, as in: Do you have a brother? I don't have any money.
And *do* itself can be a main verb, and take auxiliaries:
What are you doing? The boys have done a lot. You may not do that.

What do these three (the modals, *have,* and *be*) have in common, other than that *do* may not appear in the same clause with them? They are all auxiliaries. Once students know this, they need to learn the partial rule that:

> *Do* never appears in the same clause
> with an auxiliary.

Once they have taken *do* out of the sentences, they should be able to see how to form the questions and negatives correctly:

> Must I take an entrance exam?
> Why can't you send two pounds?
> Has she come yet?
> Is he going?
> Never must you spit like that.
> Nowhere can you see so many people.
> I haven't gone yet.
> He isn't studying tonight.

2.1.2 Underuse in questions

This mistake is more important than others in this chapter because word order is disturbed:

> †Why we bow to each other?
> †How Americans dress themselves?

In these examples, the problem is the opposite of the one in the first section. Here *do* was left out when it should have been included, since there are no auxiliaries around. The part of the rule which applies to this group is:

> *Do* appears in questions when there is no
> auxiliary.

The *do* rule provides an interesting example of a principle of English which we stressed in Chapter 1: English has a basic major constituent word order, *subject-verb.* In all normal questions with auxiliaries, the preferred *subject-verb* is preserved because the English inversion rule switches the first auxiliary with the subject. But if there is no auxiliary in the clause, *do* comes in and is inverted with the subject so as to preserve the *subject-verb* order:

> Why can't you send the package today?
> Must I take this medicine?
> Do you hear something in the cellar?

We gave two questions where *do* was missing above, and they can be corrected simply by insertion of *do*:

> Why do we bow to each other?
> How do Americans dress themselves?

Here are some similar goofs:

> †Paints the boy?
> †Go you to school?
> †When began the game?
> †There lives your teacher?

In this group too, *do* is missing. However, this group seems more un-English than the first group because the main verb has been inverted with the subject, thereby destroying the preferred *subject-verb* sequence. Students may see why *do* comes in when there is no auxiliary: so that it, and not the real verb, will be switched. That way the *subject-verb* sequence remains undisturbed:

> Does the boy paint?
> Do you go to school?
> When did the game begin?
> Does your teacher live there?

2.1.3 Overuse in affirmative sentences

One extra condition on the use of *do* can be seen from these examples:

> †I did leave yesterday.
> †He does spend his holidays always at Benin.
> †We do go to church every Sunday.
> †Our priest did give each one a cushion.

Although there is no auxiliary in any sentence, *do* does not belong. Why? Because these sentences are affirmative, not questions or negatives.

The complete rule for *do* is this:

> *Do* appears in a clause if that clause has no auxiliary and if it is a question or a negative. Otherwise *do* does not appear.[1]

2.1.4 DO missing from negatives

Students tend to insert different things between the verb and its object, including *not*:

> *Group A*
> †I practice not religion.
> †He writes not good books.
> †He saw not the beautiful lady.

Compare those goofs with this group:

> *Group B*   .
> †The horse not eats the meat.
> †Not run here.
> †I not went yesterday.

In both groups, *do* is missing, but lots of people feel the sentences in group B are easier to grasp than those in A. In A, *not* is wedged in between the verb and its object. In the B sentences, *not* precedes the *verb-object* pair. If we wedge the *not* in after the verb in the B sentences, they sound like the A group:

> *The horse eats not the meat.
> *Run not here.
> *I went not yesterday.

And these versions sound more confusing than the original B group because the *verb-object* sequence has been disturbed. Students need to learn the rule for negative placement:

---

[1]We are ignoring for the moment sentences where *do* is used for emphasis, as in:
 But I *do* like your cooking!
See the Pedagogical Notes, page 37, for some work on this form. But students should not be taught this usage until you are sure they aren't using the *do* simply to carry tense. Pretend that emphatic word order doesn't exist until the students are clear about the basic sentence forms and ready to handle stylistic deviations with care.

> *Do* appears in negatives when there is no auxiliary, and *not* follows it.[1]

This yields correct sentences:

I do not practice religion.
He does not write good books.
He did not see the beautiful lady.
The horse did not eat the meat.
Do not run here.
I did not go yesterday.

2.1.5 General rules for question and negative formation

We have seen quite a variety of mistakes which are not really so baffling if some simple rules are learned: the main verb is never inverted with the subject in questions, and *not* never comes between the verb and its object. So it seems that English has two rules, inversion and negative placement, that are part of a conspiracy to keep English word order as close to *subject-verb-object* as possible.

Experience suggests that students associate *do* with negatives and questions specifically. Goofs like this do not occur very often:

*He does can go.

Perhaps the reason is that it doesn't occur to students to insert *do* in affirmative sentences. Depending on how students have been taught English before, we might assume that they think negative sentences and questions are signalled by *do* preceding the verb. And this is not unreasonable, because most students do goof by using the *do* in questions, whether it belongs in them or not.

The most important thing for them to learn is that *do* and an auxiliary never appear together in the same clause. Here are two simple rules summarizing what we have been talking about:

> To form questions, put the question word first, if there is one, and place the first auxiliary in front of the subject.

---

[1] We are not considering other negative words, such as *never*.

> To form negatives, put *not* after the first auxiliary.

To make both of these rules work we need another rule:

> If there is no auxiliary, put in *do* and treat it as the first auxiliary.

2.1.6 Tense misplacement

You have noticed that every time we put in a *do* where it was needed we also put the tense on and made *do* agree with its subject. For example, instead of †*Paints the boy?* we tell the student to say *Does the boy paint?* not **Do the boy paints?* The reason for this is the rule that:

> Every finite clause in English has only one place for the tense: on the first verbal word.

The verbal word can be *do,* an auxiliary, or a main verb.

Remember auxiliaries are optional. That means any one, or any combination, or none, may appear in a clause. If more than one appears, they must always be in this order: *modal-have-be.* So, since tense has to go on the first verbal word, it has to go on the auxiliary if one appears. If not, and if the sentence is a question or negative, *do* comes in where the auxiliary would have been and gets tensed.

	First verbal word
The boy paints.	*main verb*
Does the boy paint?	do
Could he paint?	*auxiliary*

One of the most common mistakes students make is to put a tense on more than one verbal word:

†Why did he went?
†Does she likes it here?
†You didn't sent the form.
†Not only did I ate too much . . .
†I did not spent too much money.

Or they put in two conflicting tenses in one clause:

†Do you saw her already?
†Where does he sent it?

We feel the first group sounds better on one hearing than the second group. Perhaps this is because in the first group both tenses are the same (*did-went, does-likes, didn't-sent, did-ate, did-spent*), so the actual tense of the whole clause is not confused. All these students have to learn is that tense goes only on the first auxiliary, nothing else. That takes care of the tense for the whole clause.

However, the sentences in the second group are a little confusing because the tenses within the clause do not agree with each other. It isn't clear what tense the clause is supposed to be in; from the *do*, one expects the present tense. But then that expectation isn't fulfilled, because later in the clause one hears *saw*. Thus, it is important for the student to learn that tense goes only on the first verbal word since this gives the hearer his cue early, and removes any confusion.

Why did he go?
Does she like it here?
You didn't send the form.
Not only did I eat too much.
I did not spend too much money.
Did you see her already?
Where does he send it?

2.2 The auxiliaries HAVE and BE

2.2.1 Misformation of perfect and progressive aspects

Students often produce defective sentences like these:

†In New York I have saw Broadway.
†I have drove there before.
†We are stayed here already three weeks.
†He gone.

What is wrong with all these sentences? One thing: formation of the perfect aspect of the verb:

> The perfect aspect of the verb is a combination of some form of *have* and the past participial form of the next verbal word in the sentence.

When students know how this aspect is formed, the main problem will be for them to learn the past participial forms of the verbs. The verbal word which follows *have* must be in the participial form, whatever that form is. As shorthand for the participial form, let's use the characteristic ending *ED*. So perfect aspect can be represented as *have+ED*, which means the verbal word following *have* must come in its past participial form.

When the past participial forms are irregular, students may need to learn them carefully so as to correct their sentences:

In New York I have seen Broadway.
I have driven there before.
We have stayed here already three weeks.
How long have you been here?
He has gone.

The verb has another aspect, the progressive, which causes students trouble too:

†I thinking always of my parents and sister when it rains.
†He singing too loudly.
†He always saying that we can't do things.
†He is sleep now.
†You are drive too fast.

The big problem in all these sentences is the same: in one way or the other, the progressive aspect is not formed right.

> The progressive aspect of the verb is a combination of some form of *be* and the present participial form of the next verbal word in the sentence.

As shorthand for this, we can represent the progressive aspect as *be + ING*. The progressive is easier than the perfect aspect because students don't have to cope with irregular verbs. The present participial form of a verb is always formed by adding *ING* to the stem. So there are two possible problems – either they forget the *be* or leave off the *ING*. Students seem to forget the *be* more often than they forget the *ING*, and this may be part of a general tendency to omit *be* in its various uses.

I am thinking always of my parents and sister when it rains.
He is singing too loudly.
He is always saying that we can't do things.
He is sleeping now.
You are driving too fast.

2.2.2 Passive auxiliary misformation

Here are some other kinds of mistakes which involve *be*:

†I have impressed with Plato.
†If it hadn't been for the new government, many people would have destroyed in the grave.
†Three packages sent yesterday.
†The bread finished and he went to buy more.
†Fred's parents thought he should scolded and beaten.

The *be* that's missing in these is the one used to form passive sentences.

> The passive is a combination of some form of *be* and the past participial form of the next verbal word in the sentence.

This can be represented as *be* + *ED*, and describes normal passive sentences.

I am impressed with Plato.
If it hadn't been for the new government, many people would have been destroyed in the grave.
Three packages were sent yesterday.
The bread was finished and he went to buy more.
Fred's parents thought he should be scolded and beaten.

2.2.3 BE missing

So far, we have seen that if students have trouble with *be* the most likely thing for them to do is to omit it. This isn't surprising when you consider how many languages get along without any word corresponding to *be*. In addition to leaving out *be* in progressives and passives, students also leave it out of other kinds of sentences.

†The bus always full of people.
†John old.

†Abdul very tall.
†My mind always worried.
†He teacher.
†She borned in Izmir.
†I have three brothers. First one teacher, and other one doctor, and third engineer.

None of these sentences has a verb. Their predicates are not verbs, but adjectives, adverbs, and noun phrases. That means there is no place to put the tense. In many languages notions like *tall, here, full,* etc. are expressed by verbs. In other languages the tense can be expressed without a verbal predicate. In still others, a tense is not needed in every sentence. Teachers can expect that speakers of languages like those will have trouble remembering to use *be.* The rule for them is simple:

> Insert *be* before any predicate which is not a verb.

Examples of predicates which are not verbs are:

Adjectives: tall, full of people, cuter than a button, fat, worried, etc.
Adverbs: here, yesterday, downtown, etc.
Prepositional phrases: on the table, beneath contempt, in the city, etc.
Noun phrases: a doctor, a teacher with a car, the oldest man around, a tall man, a big door, etc.

If a subject noun phrase is not followed by a verbal word (an auxiliary, *do,* or a main verb), but by a predicate like those above, *be* is inserted. Then remaining goofs can be corrected.

The bus was always full of people.
John is old.
Abdul is very tall.
My mind was always worried.
He is teacher.
She was borned in Izmir.
I have three brothers. First one is teacher, and other one is doctor, and third is engineer.

When *be* is used, it may be preceded by any of the modals, by *have,* and by any aspect of the verb except passive.

You know that the auxiliaries, perfect, and progressive are optional. But if more than one appear, they must be in this order:

modal	*can, will, etc.*
perfect	*have + ED*
progressive	*be + ING*
passive	*be + ED*
main verb	

modal, perfect, progressive
Tom could have been being sarcastic.

modal, perfect, passive:
He might have been delayed.

progressive, passive:
They were being inspected.

modal, progressive:
She must be waiting.

Actually, students very rarely make mistakes in ordering of aspects. We have not found sentences where they put the progressive aspect before the perfect as in:

*John is having written letters all day.

2.2.4   DO misused with BE

Be cannot be preceded by *do*, as in these goofs:

†Do they be happy?
†The secretary doesn't be here today.
†He don't be here now.

Students making such goofs can be told to treat *be* as an auxiliary. Review the rules for forming questions and negatives (Section 2.1.5, page 28) and remind them not to use *do* with any auxiliary. This should enable them to see why they should say:

Are they happy?
The secretary isn't here today.
He isn't here now.

2.3 Modals

2.3.1 Misformation of the next verbal word

We have been talking about auxiliaries which have an affix associated with them. The perfect has *ED*, the progressive has ING, and the passive has *ED*. The modals, however, have no affix associated with them. There are no forms like *can seeing,* or *should written,* although these forms come up in student speech:

†I can going if you can.
†We should studying tonight.
†Our priest can leaving soon.
†They should left.
†He must written it.

Since affixes that belong with other auxiliaries always go with the next verbal word, and since modals have no affix:

> Any verbal word immediately following a modal is naked, that is, has no ending at all.

I can go if you can.
We should study tonight.
Our priest can leave soon.
They should leave. *or* They should have left.
He must write it. *or* He must have written it.

Not only do modals rule out affixes on the following verbal word, they will not tolerate a mediating *to* before an infinitive either. But some of the most frequent goofs are:

†I can to go.
†I should to read English all the time.

Though this is not a devastating goof, it can combine with pronunciation problems to cause confusion. For example, *I can to go* may sound like *I can't go.*

Students may be confusing modals with non-modal verbs such as *want to* or *ought to.* They need to learn the list of modals, and that:

> Modals do not take *to* before a following infinitive.

This yields correct sentences:

I can go.
I should read English all the time.

2.3.2 Misunderstanding of tense with modals

Modals are inherently tensed. Tense is an inseparable part of each modal and because of this, they have the same limitations as explicitly tensed verbal words like *goes, likes, went.*[1]

What are these limitations? First of all, modals can't have any sort of inflection. We can no more say **musting* than **walkeding*, or **coulds* than **walkeds*. As you know, tense must go on the first verbal word in the clause. So, since modals are already inherently tensed:

> Modals must come before any other verbal word if they appear at all.

As far as we have observed, students don't tend to violate this rule too often. Sentences like these are extremely rare:

†You have could do it if you wanted to.
†No one is may leaving now.

However, if students say these things the rule above is the one for them to learn.

You could do it if you wanted to.
No one may leave now.

But sometimes we hear:

†I must can catch this train.
†You must will send me money.

---

[1]The only forms modals come in are these:

Present tense modals	*Past tense modals*
can	could
shall	should
will	would
may	might
must	

The "past tense" of a modal is not semantically like the past tense of a real verb. That is, the relationship between *can* and *could* is not like that between *walk* and *walked*.

†We shall can leave tomorrow, isn't it?
†I should must going tomorrow.

But we know that only one verbal word per clause is tensed. So, since modals are inherently tensed:

> Only one modal may appear in any clause, and no verbal word after the modal may be tensed.

Otherwise there would be two words tensed in the clause, a situation logically just like **I wanted helped him.*

I must catch this train.
You will send me money.
We shall leave tomorrow, isn't it?
I should go tomorrow.

2.4 Mismatching auxiliaries in tag questions

Often we hear goofs like these:

†She has been smoking less, isn't it?
†He won't come tonight, is it?
†You like French brandy, isn't it?

The rule to pass on to these students is simple:

> The auxiliary in the tag must be the same as the first auxiliary in the main clause. If there is no auxiliary in the main clause, *do* is used in the tag.

She has been smoking less, hasn't she?
He won't come tonight, will he?
You like French brandy, don't you?

PEDAGOGICAL NOTES

2.5 Contradictions

An excellent way of flexing all sorts of auxiliary muscles along with teaching something useful in itself is to teach the students how to contradict you. To practice, make up lots of outrageous statements that they will have to contradict. The beauty of this is that, unlike drills, this method exploits the real situations where these sentences would normally be said. The contradictory device we have in mind for emphatic sentences this:

> Stress the first auxiliary in emphatic affirmative replies.

Begin with outrageous negative statements, so that students will have to answer in the affirmative.

For example, if when surveying the room you see John, say:

> I see that John isn't here again today.

His reply should be:

> I *am* here!

And if the sentence has no auxiliary, students will have to put in *do*, as in questions and negatives without auxiliaries, to make their point. For example, you might tell a student:

> Well, since you never like holidays . . .

Any self-respecting student would instantly reply:

> But I *do* like holidays!

One of the benefits of this method is that it is a good way of getting into the normal intonation pattern — practicing supression of all but the emphasized word. Furthermore, through this practice the students learn about the emphatic *do* in affirmative sentences in proper perspective.

There is a corresponding positive sentence which is an alternative to simply stressing the first auxiliary:

> *Cue:*   You won't finish that job today.
>
> *Response:*   I will $^{so}_{too}$ finish it.

The *so* or *too* actually reinforces the students' consciousness of the auxiliary because of the rule:

> Stress *so* or *too* which goes after the first auxiliary.[1]

---

[1]The examples with *so* and *too* are more typical of children's speech, and may sound belligerent in adult speech.

You can introduce other forms which stress the first auxiliary and the elicit questions.

Repairman: "I can't possibly come over today."
Housewife: "Well, when *can* you come, anyway?"

One woman: "She didn't marry him for his money."
Other woman: "Well, why *did* she marry him, then?"

The point of all this is to keep the students operating with the auxiliary.

Now if you goad the student with a positive outrageous statement, he has to reply with a negative, which will be stressed in one of two ways:

> If *not* is present, it gets the stress. If it is contracted, the verb to which it is attached gets the stress.

For example, suppose you say:

It's way past your bedtime.

The student should reply:

It's *not way past my bedtime.* or
It *isn't* way past my bedtime.

Situations like this are easy to invent.

2.6 Headline decipherment

If your students tend to omit *be*, try teaching them headline decipherment, a problem in itself for learners. Explain that headlines are usually abbreviations of full sentences, and that *be*, generally in its present or present perfect form, is frequently omitted.[1] Select a batch of headlines with *be* missing and have the students reconstruct the full sentences.

PRISONERS UNION FORMED UPSTATE	*A* Prisoners' Union *has been* formed upstate.	*passive*

---

[1]As sometimes are articles and relative pronouns with *be* (...*who is* ...), and occasionally other words.

BUSINESS COMPLAIN-ING ABOUT CONTROLS	Business *is* complaining about *the* controls.	*progressive*
PRESIDENT CRANKY OVER CRITICS	*The* President *is* cranky over *his* critics.	*adjective*
CRITICS A MAJOR OBSTRUCTION TO NEGOTIATIONS SAYS MEDIATOR	"*The* critics *are* a major obstruction to negotiations," says *the* mediator.	*noun phrase*

In these sample headlines, *be* must be restored to form the passive, progressive, and adjective and noun phrase predicates. Of course, you would choose headlines so as to give your students practice with the constructions which most often trouble them.

Headlines can become quite a puzzle when they pile one *be*-ellipsis onto another.

TWO MORE JAPANESE EX-SOLDIERS REPORTED SIGHTED ON GUAM.	Two more Japanese ex-soldiers *are* reported *to have been* sighted on Guam.
QUEEN ELIZABETH REPORTED GOING INTO MOTHBALLS.	*The* Queen Elizabeth *has been* reported *to be* going into mothballs.

2.7 Memorization of modals

The modals present one case where there is no getting away from memorizing a list. Fortunately, it's a short one:

Present tense modals	*Past tense modals*
can	could
shall	should
will	would
may	might
must	

Here the student of English as a second language is in the same boat as a child learning English as his first language. Both make mistakes indicating they aren't sure which words are modals.

If you notice that a student consistently handles certain modals correctly, but makes mistakes with others, he probably needs to memorize the list. This may be the case especially if he uses words that aren't modals as if they were:

    †I need find my application.
    †Want you come to my house today?

2.8 Correction of free conversation

We can't utter questions or negatives without an auxiliary or its surrogate *do*. So any time that you teach or drill those structures, you are also teaching the use of the auxiliary system, even though you may be concentrating on other matters such as inversion in questions, the use of *some* and *any,* or the difference between *no* and *not*.

Fortunately, questions and negatives come up constantly in conversation, so it is easy to find occasions to correct them in context.

CHAPTER 3

PASSIVE SENTENCES

DEFINITIONS

Before we discuss the various kinds of mistakes students make with passive sentences, the words passive and active should be clear. These are actually very simple notions which do not often receive attention. But they are essential for understanding student mistakes.

"Active" is an adjective that applies to a person or animal regarded as doing something, such as causing, moving, or changing something or someone. It is also natural to think of inanimate objects of certain kinds as active, such as vehicles or tools used to move or change something. "Passive" is an adjective that applies to a person or animal who is undergoing, feeling the effects of, or being the victim of someone or something else's action. The passive one is not doing anything himself.

The active and passive participants in an event are represented grammatically. The active participant is traditionally called the agent. If a verb denotes an action, its agent is generally represented grammatically as the subject of the sentence. So it appears first in the sentence. The passive participant, on the other hand, is grammatically the object of the verb or of a preposition. So it appears after the verb. *Subject-verb-object* is the natural order in active sentences, as we saw in Chapter 1.

subject	verb	object
(agent)	*(active verb)*	
My brother	finished	the paint job.

But English has a device for reorganizing active sentences so that the passive participant, which would be the direct object in an active sentence, shows up as the subject. This means putting the verb in its passive form as well as changing the word order. And it is done for various reasons, such as to use the object as the topic of the sentence, or to avoid mentioning the agent.

subject	verb	
	(passive verb)	(agent)
The paint job	was finished.	
The paint job	was finished	by my brother.

The terms active and passive apply basically to noun phrases, describing their mode of participation or their role in an event. These notions are extended to verbs also. A verb is called active in its form if its subject is active, that is, if the subject is the agent. The verb is called passive in its form if its subject is passive, that is, if the subject is not the agent but the passive participant. And these notions are also extended to sentences.

For every full passive sentence with *by* and the agent, then, there is a corresponding active one which expresses the same idea. For example, here is an active sentence:

> The ball hit Eliphas on the elbow.   *active*

It has as its passive equivalent:

> Eliphas was hit on the elbow by the ball.   *passive*

If one asks who was hit, or what hit whom, the answers are the same in both sentences. The grammatical relations are the same; since both answer questions about who do what whom in the same way, even though the sentences don't look identical.

The first four sections below will analyse problems students have in forming passive sentences. The remaining sections discuss examples where the passive should not have been used at all.

ANALYSIS OF GOOF TYPES

3.1 Problems with formation of passive sentences

3.1.1 Misformation of passive verb

> †The bread finished.
> †Each cushion given by our priest.
> †I have impressed greatly with the ideas of Plato.
> †They have invited and they came.
> †I have so disappointed with you.

†The hymn was singing so beautiful.
†There were many things which were practicing, such
as thuggery, bribery and disturbance.

Students who say these sentences must learn this rule for
passive formation:

> The passive auxiliary *be* must precede the
> predicate verb which is in its past participial
> *ED* form.

There is extended discussion of this sort of mistake in
Chapter 2, Section 2.2.2 (page 32).

The bread is finished.
Each cushion was given by our priest.
I have been impressed greatly with the ideas of Plato.
They were invited and they came.
I have been so disappointed with you.
The hymn was sung so beautiful.
There were many things which were practiced, such
as thuggery, bribery and disturbance.

3.1.2 Active order but passive form

The problem with these goofs is much less mechanical, and
more destructive for communication; they are global.

†The traffic jam was held up my brother.
†The principal was looked into the students' proposal.
†Alex was enjoyed the party very much.
†The government was forbidden the people to grow
opium.

In such cases, what your students meant and what their
common goofs are will determine the type of correction. If
they often have trouble forming simple past tenses, and tend
to insert *be* when it doesn't belong, then merely correcting
the tenses to simple past active forms will suffice.

However, perhaps they do not usually misform active
sentences by inserting an extra *be*, and you know from what
they mean that the correct passive sentences would be
appropriate. Then their problem is that the rule in Section
3.1.1 has been applied and the verb is in its passive form, but
the subject (agent) and object of each sentence are still in the

active order. So the next point about forming passive sentences is:

> The agent in a passive sentence cannot remain the subject. Instead, the first noun phrase after the active verb becomes the subject.

This rule, which is much more important for comprehension than that in Section 3.1.1, produces correct passive word order:

	agent removed
My brother was held up.	the traffic jam
The student's proposal was looked into.	the principal
The party was enjoyed very much.	Alex
The people were forbidden to grow opium.	the government

3.1.3 Absent or wrong preposition before agent

In active sentences, the agent announces its role by coming first in the sentence. If it is simply inserted by itself into a passive sentence, however, the result sounds awful:

†My brother was held up the traffic jam.

A noun phrase right after a verb is always interpreted as a direct object, so the roles of who does what to whom are unclear. When the agent is not first, it must be signalled by the preposition *by* in front of it. It then follows the passive verb preceded by that *by*, which says; "this noun phrase is the agent." So the rule here is:

> The agent in a passive sentence must have the preposition *by* in front of it.

My brother was held up by the traffic jam.
The student's proposal was looked into by the principal.
The party was enjoyed very much by Alex.
The people were forbidden by the government to grow opium.

Even if the verb is not in passive form, but the object and

subject have been permuted or switched around, *by* still clears up the meaning:

†The party enjoyed by Alex very much.
†My brother held up by the traffic jam.
†The students' proposal looked into by
the principal.
†The people forbidden by the government
to grow opium.

And this is because the roles of the agent and subject are made clear by having *by* precede the agent. After that has been learned, students can be taught to insert the correct form of *be*.

Sometimes students put in a preposition, but the wrong one:

†She is not allowed to her parents to go.
†We are not wanted at him.
†The news was told from our teacher. He said . . .

Learning to make consistent use of *by* should clear up this kind of goof.

She is not allowed by her parents to go.
We are not wanted by him.
The news was told by our teacher. He said . . .

3.1.4 Passive order but active form

Here is yet another type of goof which looks like a failure to use the passive when it should be used. This type is global, like that in Section 3.1.2, page 44.

†English use many countries.
†Everything covered insurance against fire.
†These lessons need freshmen.

The trouble is that the subject and object have been switched around. The word order is appropriate to the passive, but the verb is in the active form.

There is more than one way to correct these goofs. If the major constituents are left in the same order, we must passivize the verb, and add *by* to signal the agent. Or we can simply put the major constituents in their proper order, *subject-verb-object*. Which correction you teach depends on what you believe the students mean, and on their dialect, as discussed above in Section 3.1.2.

passive		*active*
English is used by many	*or*	Many countries use
countries.		English.
Everything was covered	*or*	Insurance against fire
by insurance against fire.		covered everything.
These lessons are needed	*or*	Freshmen need these
by freshmen.		lessons.

3.2. Inappropriate use of passive

3.2.1 Making intransitive verbs passive

†I hope that the good will between U.S.A. and Republic of Korea *will be lasted* long time.
†Some people afraid that if the war ends a financial crisis *will be arisen.*
†He *was arrived* early.

Look at the italicized parts of these examples. Verbs like *last, arise,* and *arrive* are intransitive and that means objects may not follow them. But the idea of passive sentences in English is to put the object of the verb or another noun phrase in subject position. If there is no object of the verb or of a preposition, there is no noun phrase to become the subject of the passive verb. So the sequence *be* plus the past participial *ED* form of the verb may not appear.

> An active verb which is to be made passive must be followed by a noun phrase.

I hope that the good will between U.S.A. and Republic of Korea will last long time.
Some people afraid that if the war ends a financial crisis will arise.
He arrived early.

The noun phrase can be the object of a preposition, as in the following sentences:

The principal looked *into* the students' proposal.	*active*
The students' proposal was looked *into.*	*passive*

It looks as though someone has   *active*
stepped *on* this plum.
It looks as though this plum has   *passive*
been stepped *on*.

3.2.2 Misusing passives in complex sentences

†I was suggested by Mrs. Sena to forget about
this project.
†We were recommended by her to spend less
money.

Here the student has taken the subject of one clause in a
complex sentence and made it the subject of the other clause.
Syntactically these are global errors and should be corrected
early because they confuse the relation between clauses. The
rule is:

> The passive operation applies only within
> single clauses.

The student sentences are complex, with two clauses each,
and must be left active. *That* can be used:

Clause 1	*Clause 2*
Mrs. Sena suggested	that I forget about this project.
She recommended	that we spend less money.

It is easy to see then that the student goofs were formed by
taking the subject of the second clause and putting it into the
first clause.

These goofs are complicated because students often don't
know what kind of complements go with verbs like
recommend and *suggest*. The whole issue of complementation of these and similar verbs will be discussed at
length in Chapter 5, Section 5.3.6, page 91.

We found one other example of this type:

†Mark was hoped to become a football player.

There are two likely sources of such a goof.[1] If the student
simply hasn't learned how to put an active sentence into the

---

[1] A third possibility, confusion over the meaning of *hope*, is discussed in Section
3.6, page 53.

past tense, the correction would be:

Mark hoped to become a football player.

But perhaps the student meant to say:

Clause 1	Clause 2
Someone hoped	that Mark would become a football player.

We can see that he made the same goof as in the earlier examples, taking the subject out of the second clause and putting it in the first clause when making a passive.

It is possible to use the passive construction in sentences like that above, but a special device is used, the little word *it*. If we take the sentence and passivize it as it stands, we have:

That Mark would become a football player was hoped (by someone).

But English speakers prefer not to put such big, or fat, clauses in initial positions. So if a student wants to use the passive, he can insert *it* as representative of the fat clause in the subject position, or surrogate subject, and leave the fat clause at the end of the sentence:

It was hoped that Mark would become a football player.

This way of using *it* when subjects threaten to be too large is quite common in English. If the subject is too fat, we use the passive to get it out of the way.

It was thought that he would never return.
She's being chased by the fattest man I know.

PEDAGOGICAL NOTES

3.3. Scrambling

Putting words on cards and having students string them together is a method that can be used for teaching the correct form of passive sentences. Words like *by*, past participles, and forms of the auxiliary *be* can serve as cues for passive sentences.

Such cards might look like these:

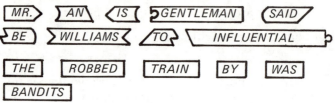

3.4 Substitution drills

Another way to practice the correct form of passive sentences is to have students fill slots. As with other drills, it will be most effective to wait with slot-filling exercises until you actually hear a goof. For example, if a student uses a wrong verb form, write his sentence on the board, point out the offending word, and have the class fill in other words in the correct form in that slot.

†The bread almost using up.

Cue:	The bread _____ almost _____.
Responses:	The bread was almost used up.
	is almost baked.
	was almost dropped. (etc.)

To help teach the past participial forms, both regular and irregular, an example sentence might be:

The ball was _____ by Stephen
   kicked
   rolled
   stepped on
   hit
   lost
   thrown
   put away (etc.)

To practice the presence of *be*, students can fill in the correct forms in sentences like this:

The child _____ kissed by the queen.
   children
   girl (etc.)

Subjects can be plural or singular, and the present, past, and future tenses can be practiced in this way.

The whole passive verb construction can also be practiced with slots:

The ball team _____ _____ by the _____

was	challenged	next town
is	supported	Chamber of Commerce
will be	questioned	manager

And if students have trouble with the preposition *by*, that slot can be left blank so they can practice it, especially if they tend to leave it out after other prepositions.

We were _____ Mrs. Johnson.

invited by
told stories by
taught French by
talked to by
argued with by
looked at by

3.5 Role playing

Generally, the passive is used when for one reason or another the speaker wants to leave out or deemphasize the agent. The speaker may want to shirk responsibility, when the subject would otherwise be *I*, or may not know or care who the agent is. Students may be told that to call attention to someone, we put that someone first, even if we have to use the passive. And to distract attention from someone, we put that someone last or omit him altogether, even if we have to use the passive.

Getting the students to act out situations in which they choose between active and passive responses can make learning lively and interesting. A teacher can present a situation and offer both kinds of responses, active and passive, to the student who then chooses one.

Gestures are very effective with these. For example, when one is shirking responsibility, one's head or eyes are usually down, and one's arms hang down. But when announcing a personal victory, one's eyes are level and one's arms may be waving. To mix gestures of defeat and guilt (or of optimism and pride) with the wrong kinds of statements is often amusing.

Discussing and acting out situations where the passive is natural and colloquial can be used to motivate the somewhat tedious job of learning to form passives correctly.

Situation: Someone you aren't interested in calls up and asks you out for the dance. Two possible responses are:
    I'm sorry, but I've already been invited.
    No, Henry has already invited me.
The passive response is less devastating and gives the feeling that you really could not help the situation. And it also does not reveal whom you're going with.

Situation: You are at the airport with a friend and the plane is ready to leave. Two remarks might be:
    Hurry up! Mrs. Smith has just announced your plane.
    Hurry up! Your plane has just been announced.
The passive is more likely, since you usually don't know or care exactly who is making the announcements.

Situation: A student has won a prize in a raffle and wants to tell everyone about it:
    Guess what! I've won that car they were raffling!
    Guess what! That car they were raffling has been won
    by me!
Since the point is to call attention to the agent and his luck, the active sentence is more suitable. Other situations where the active is used to focus on the subject are easy to invent.

Situation: Your boss comes back from a three-week vacation, and you haven't done very much while he was gone. He asks you:
    Well, what did you accomplish while I was gone?
Two responses are:
    Sorry, I didn't accomplish too much because I
    had a lot of problems.
    Well, not too much was accomplished because
    a lot of problems came up.
The passive response gives less direct responsibility to the speaker than the active one.

Situation: You are examining a winter coat you have just pulled out of the closet and thinking about it. You could say:

    This coat should be cleaned.
    Someone should clean this coat.

When a sentence contains both a definite and indefinite noun, most people prefer to emphasize the definite one (*coat*) by making it the subject, as in the first alternative.

3.6 Finding out what students mean

When a student makes goofs in free conversation, the teacher should know what he intends to say in order to understand what his mistake actually is. Questions can help determine this. For example, suppose a student says:

†The girl was decided to play the piano.

You can ask questions like:

Who decided? The girl or someone else?

If the student answers *the girl*, then he doesn't know how to form an active sentence in its past tense. (Section 3.1.2, page 44). *Be* is not used, and the sentence is simply:

The girl decided to play the piano.

But if the agent was intended to be *someone else*, even someone unknown, he has taken a subject out of another clause in forming his passive. (Section 3.2.2., page 48) Then he meant:

Someone decided that the girl should play the piano.

Show him that there are two clauses in this sentence, and that subjects cannot be taken out of one clause and put in another when passives are being formed. That is, *the girl* is the subject of the second clause and must remain there rather than being shifted into the first clause.

There is a third possibility, that the student does not know the correct meaning and use of *decide*. Perhaps he thinks *decide, hope, suggest* and *recommend* are like *persuade, encourage* and *tell*. In that case, it isn't passive formation that the student needs to learn, but the fact that *decide* and the others don't work like *persuade*; they do not make animate objects (that can do or experience things, living beings), and so in this context cannot be made passive (Section 3.2.1, page 47). We can say:

We persuaded the girl to play the piano.
The girl was persuaded to play the piano.

We encouraged her to play.
She was encouraged to play.

But we cannot say:

*We decided her.
*We hoped her.
*We suggested her.

Students who frequently have difficulty with this kind of goof may need to work intensively on verb complementation, which is discussed in Chapter 5, Section 5.3.6, page 91.

CHAPTER 4

TEMPORAL CONJUNCTIONS

There are various types of conjunctions (coordinate, causal, temporal) that are commonly used in English, but we will discuss only temporal conjunctions here. The greatest emphasis will be placed on those temporal conjunctions that cause students the most trouble.

The very basic global goofs of attaching a temporal conjunction to the wrong clause or misforming the subordinate clause make many student sentences hard to understand. These goofs and others are often made because the students don't know the meaning of the conjunctions, so we will introduce this chapter by presenting a set of systematic definitions which contain the information needed for correcting the goofs. The definitions will enable the teacher to locate the source of a goof and provide a way of explaining the goof to the student. And since the definitions depend on an understanding of limited and unlimited verbs, we will start by examining those.

Other basic problems with temporal conjunctions include verb selection and tense sequence in the clauses, and the dropping of *will* and *that*. Some of these can be explained by general rules. But there are certain idiosyncrasies in the tense sequence requirements that do not seem to follow any particular rules. Any idiosyncratic information about each conjunction will accompany its definition. Throughout the analysis we will present the teacher with some guides for ordering correction of student mistakes based on their importance for comprehension and their importance for exposing other goofs.

We must stress that this chapter is not as complete in its analysis as the other chapters. It points to as many unanswered questions as it presents "solutions" to problems.

DEFINITIONS

4.1. Limited and unlimited verbs

Many errors which students make with temporal conjunctions can be traced to a single source. Let's consider the relevant goof types in simple sentences:

†Please know the address for me.
†I asked him to know everything.
†Why don't you go and have a car?
†Where did you have your beautiful wife?
†I'm coming; I only have to finish wearing my kimono.
†First keep away your books and then line up by the door.
†He was rich by gambling.

The distinction these students are missing is that between limited and unlimited verbs, terms that have to do with the time span of the verb.

The basic distinction here is that unlimited verbs describe "states of being" (*have, know*), and limited verbs describe "getting there" (*get, find out*). Unlimited (U) verbs describe states or actions that continue for some time. They have no explicit beginning or end point in themselves. Limited (L) verbs describe events that are finite in time. They are understood to have a beginning and an end. Often they are brief actions.[1]

Unlimited verbs—U	*Limited verbs—L*
	Pairs frequently confused
know	find out, learn
have	get, receive
be	become, get (+*participial form*)
wear	put on
sit	sit down
keep	put
sleep	fall asleep

Other common verbs

intend	stay	decide	finish
remain	need	drop	lose
want	hate	happen	begin
like	go on	admire	succeed
continue	study	sneeze	arrive
wait	work	wake up	build

---

[1]Verbs are considered inherently limited or unlimited, which means they have this characteristic in the simple tenses—past, present, and future. We will show later how these inherent qualities can be changed by using the progressive aspect or other devices. (Sections 4.5.2-4.5.3, pages 68-71).

One of the most important vocabulary lessons is the difference between *be* and *become*. In terms of this distinction, students can understand the relation between other U "being" and L "getting there" pairs like *have* and *get, know* and *find out,* and so on. This lexical distinction is often troublesome for students whose native languages use one verb to express both the unlimited and the limited notions. There are also languages which have a regular morphological process, such as an inflection or change of form of the word, to express the distinction. Students speaking such languages might be searching for an inflection of *know* instead of realizing that they must use a totally different word like *learn* or *find out.*

> Please find out the address for me.
> I asked him to learn everything.
> Why don't you go and get a car?
> Where did you meet your beautiful wife?
> I'm coming; I only have to finish putting on my kimono.
> First put away your books and then line up by the door.
> He got rich by gambling.

4.2. Major temporal conjunctions

We do not claim that the definitions given here are complete in their information about each conjunction, but rather that the information included goes a long way toward correcting many of the major goof types we have observed.

Each conjunction selects certain semantic features which must appear in the clauses it joins. Its meaning and the selectional information about each conjunction will be discussed and summed up into a concise definition which may serve as a shorthand for the analysis of goofs. These will also bring out the distinctions between the conjunctions more clearly.[1]

There are two situations which we do not take into account in these definitions, the negative and the perfect

---

[1] With respect to selection, we will only specify those features that are required. If there is free choice about some feature in one of the clauses, it will not be discussed at length.

aspect, especially the past perfect, as we understand too little about how these interact with limited and unlimited verbs. (*Negative* is used here in its semantic sense, and includes sentences with adverbs like *hardly, seldom,* and *only* which don't have *not* or *no.* We give a partial discussion of how negatives affect temporal clauses in Section 4.5.3.)

4.2.1 BEFORE

With *before,* the earlier event or state of affairs, E1, is expressed in the main clause, and the later event, E2, in the subordinate clause. All combinations of limited (L) and unlimited (U) verbs in either clause are possible.

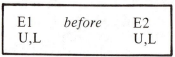

Here are some examples and diagrams of the possibilities:

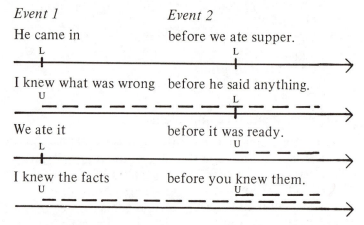

4.2.2 AFTER

After is roughly the converse of *before,* but not all sentences using *before* can be reversed to make *after* sentences. This is because *after* can only take a limited verb in the subordinate E1 clause.

Thus with *after* there is no possibility of the time spans of E1 and E2 overlapping. Here are the possibilities:

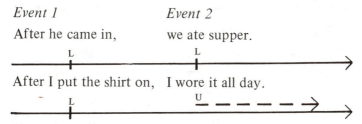

Event 1   *Event 2*

After he came in,   we ate supper.

After I put the shirt on,   I wore it all day.

4.2.3 UNTIL

Until is often confused with *before,* perhaps because they answer similar questions about E1. *Before* answers "When?" while *until* answers "How long?" However, *until* demands that E1 be unlimited, and indicates that E1 goes on just until E2 begins.

E1	*until*	E2
U		L,U

E2 marks the end of the state referred to in E1.

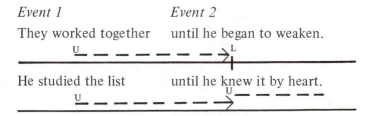

Event 1   *Event 2*

They worked together   until he began to weaken.

He studied the list   until he knew it by heart.

4.2.4 WHILE

This conjunction and *when* both relate events which are to some extent simultaneous and which overlap in time. There is not a clear sequence of E1 and E2 as with the other conjunctions, but often one event both begins and ends while the other is continuing. We will call the continuing event E1 (cont) and the interrupting or shorter one E2 (int). *While* is always attached to the clause that tells about the continuing event.

E2 (int)	*while*	E1 (cont)
U,L		U

Both E1 and E2 are understood to be passing, temporary events when they flank *while*. It is natural to interpret the continuing E1 as representing the event which lasts longer.

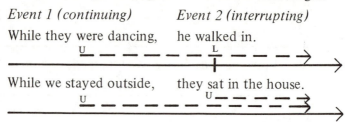

Event 1 (continuing)   *Event 2 (interrupting)*

While they were dancing,   he walked in.

While we stayed outside,   they sat in the house.

4.2.5 WHEN

When also relates events which overlap in time, but they need not be passing or temporary.

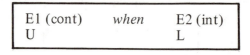

Event 1 (continuing)   *Event 2 (interrupting)*

They were dancing   when he walked in.

But *when* is more frequently used, similarily to *after* and *while*, to introduce the E1 clause. The verbs in such cases can be limited or unlimited. If the two verbs are limited, *when* (in contrast with *after*) suggests that there is almost no time lapse between the events.

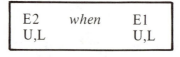

Event 1   *Event 2*

When he heard the news,   he jumped to his feet.

When I was in Holland,   I learned Dutch.

When we saw the headline,   we wanted to know more.

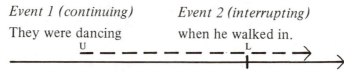

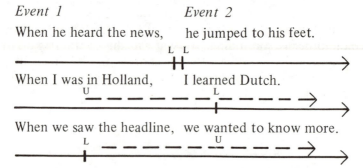

Event 1
When he was young,

Event 2
he was short for his age.

4.2.6 SINCE

With *since,* as with *after,* E1 is expressed in the subordinate clause. However, E2 does not simply follow E1 in time, but E2 is a state which began when E1 happened and continued after E1 had happened. E2 must be in the present perfect, and E1 must be in the present perfect or the past.[1] This may be because *since* relates two events that do not simply occur one after the other, but which began together at some point in the past, and of which at least one is still continuing now. *Since* differs from all the other temporal conjunctions in having this meaning.[2]

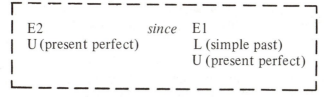

E2	*since*	E1
U (present perfect)		L (simple past)
		U (present perfect)

The meaning of *since* can be illustrated with the help of this diagram:

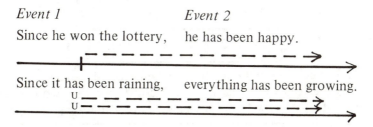

Event 1

Since he won the lottery,

Event 2

he has been happy.

Since it has been raining,   everything has been growing.

---

[1]We specifically exclude from consideration here the use of *since* as a causative conjunction, when it can take other tenses:

Since you're here, we'll begin.

[2]The rule as given is a white lie, as sometimes E2 can be limited:

Since I last saw you, I have finished three novels.

But the use of limited verbs in E2 is restricted, under circumstances difficult to define, so we will leave the definition as it is.

ANALYSIS OF GOOF TYPES

4.3 Misplacement of conjunctions

If placement of conjunctions is a problem, we suggest you correct that first, since this global mistake can make sentences really hard to understand. Also, the definitions of the conjunctions use terms like Event 1 and Event 2, so the conjunction must be attached to the right clause if this information is to be helpful.

In the event that the student associates a conjunction with the wrong clause, the definition of the conjunction is what he may need to learn most. There is no reason to expect that he will attach all conjunctions to the wrong clauses if he misattaches one, but this is a possibility.

4.3.1 AFTER

†I got up after I brushed my teeth.
†He went to Fitche to buy cloth. After he sold
the cloth and made much money.

Here you might be tempted to replace *after* with *afterwards,* but that isn't always enough, so students must learn how *after* itself relates events. Both of the clauses in a sentence with *after* represent events, preceding another in time. *After* is used to tell the order of the events. It is always the earlier event, E1. Students who make goofs like the above must learn this about the meaning of *after*.

Event 2	*after*	Event 1

And they should know that the rule for placement of *after* must be followed regardless of the order of the two clauses. They may also, without any change in meaning say:

After	Event 1,	Event 2

You might have them point out which event happened first, and tell them to attach *after* to that clause. For instance, in the first example, the event *I got up* happened before *I brushed my teeth,* so *after* should be attached to the front of *I got up.*

Then they should correct the sentences using either form:

> After I got up, I brushed my teeth.
> After he went to Fitche to buy cloth, he sold
> the cloth and made much money.

4.3.2 SINCE

> †He broke his leg since he has thrown away his skis.
> †He started to go to school. Since he has studied
> very hard.

In these examples too, the students must learn how *since* relates the two events in the sentence.

Event 2	*since*	Event 1
Since	Event 1,	Event 2

Since means that the time of the first event marks the beginning of the second event. *Since,* like *after,* is attached to Event 1. *He broke his leg* happened before *He has thrown away his skis,* and *since* must be attached to the clause that happened first:

> Since he broke his leg, he has thrown away his skis.
> He has studied very hard since he started to go to school.

4.3.3 WHILE

> †While Getachew knocked on the door, I was
> doing my homework.
> †While you can't come in, I'm in here.

While also relates two events but it's a little more complex. One event does not simply precede the other in time. *"While Event 1"* defines a time span during which Event 2 happens, so Event 1 must be able to continue for some time. Otherwise, Event 2 could not take place while Event 1 was still going on. Many times Event 2 is an interrupting event, one that does not cover a long time span. In any case, it does not cover a longer time span than Event 1.

Event 2 (interrupts)	*while*	Event 1 (continues)
While Event 1 (continues),		Event 2 (interrupts)

Knocking on the door is usually a brief act (especially in the simple past), and doing homework takes some time. *While* always is attached to the clause that tells about the continuing event: in this case, doing the homework.

In the second example, the continuing event is *I'm in here,* so *while* should be attached to that.

> Getachew knocked on the door while I was doing my homework.
> While I'm in here, you can't come in.

Another possibility is that students confuse *while* with *because.*

4.4 Form of clauses after temporal conjunctions

4.4.1 Non-finiteness of subordinate clauses

There are some goofs students make with all temporal conjunctions, and the remedy is essentially the same for them all. Here are some examples:

> †After him goes, we will read a story.
> †He will give us money before leaves.
> †After to study, you must visit your father.
> †Since that saw it, he is very sorry.

In each of these examples, the form of the clause following the subordinate conjunction is wrong in one way or another.

Perhaps the most important point to get across to these students is the following rule:

> Subordinate clauses are all finite.

This means they must have a nominative subject, and a verb which agrees with the subject and is tensed. In the examples above, the clauses following the conjunctions are not finite. Either the subject is missing, or it is not in its nominative form, or the form of the verb is wrong. To help students avoid these goofs, tell them the rule above.[1]

---

[1] They will never be wrong if they follow this rule after temporal conjunctions, even though there are certain special cases where gerunds can follow temporal conjunctions:

> After getting rid of the evidence, he ran away.

But in these cases, full finite clauses can follow just as well:

> After he got rid of the evidence, he ran away.

Applying the rule to make subordinate clauses finite, the students can then correct most of the goofs above:

After he goes, we will read a story.	*subject made nominative*
He will give us money before he leaves.	*subject added*
After we study, you must visit your father.	*verb form corrected*
Since that he saw it, he's very sorry.	*subject added*

It is important to teach them this rule early if students say things like:

†After leaves . . .
†Because he tall . . .
†Since he leave . . .
†Until him went . . .

First, the notion of a finite clause has a very general application throughout English grammar. Second, the notion helps them to learn about tense sequences associated with the temporal conjunctions. These would not make sense if students did not understand that the verbs in subordinate clauses should have a tense in the first place.

Some students make mistakes like this:

†John sleeps a lot after eats a lot.

They may be misunderstanding coordinate conjunction reduction, which permits this kind of subject deletion:

John sleeps a lot and eats a lot.

They must then learn that subjects are not dropped after temporal subordinate conjunctions:

John sleeps a lot after he eats a lot.

4.4.2 Superfluous THAT

Another, though minor, goof is the insertion of a superfluous *that* right after the temporal conjunction.

†Since that he has seen her, he has been cheerful.
†After that we walked, we felt very warm.

†He married Ketcha after that he got rich.
†Let's go to see him while that he is here.

Students eventually have to learn that:

> Subordinate conjunctions are never followed by *that*.[1]

Many other clauses, such as those following verbs like *know* and *believe,* are preceded by *that* and are also finite, but temporal conjunctions are only followed by their finite clauses, with no other connectors.

But it is not important to correct this goof early, especially since the presence of the superfluous *that* may help remind the student to make the clause finite. Whether the presence of *that* is disruptive depends on whether it is stressed or not. Consider this goof:

†He brushed his teeth after *that* he got up.

If *that* is a small, unstressed syllable, as it would be in a sentence like *I know that he's here,* this is a minor local goof for comprehension. But if *that* is stressed, it sounds like a different thing:

†He brushed his teeth after that he got up.

Pronounced this way, it becomes a global goof and can't be overlooked.

The local goofs are easily corrected:

Since he has seen her, he has been cheerful.
After we walked, we felt very warm.
He married Ketcha after he got rich.
Let's go to see him while he is here.

4.5 Selection of predicate types

4.5.1 Confusion in unlimited and limited verb selection

The limited-unlimited distinction accounts for some goofs with temporal conjunctions.

†He got rich until he married.
†I lost my wallet until Juan gave it back.

[1]Except when *that* acts as a pronoun: *After that, we left.*

†He put on his clean shirt after he wanted to go.
†After Robert kept his coat on the hook, he sat
down to eat.

We used the limited-unlimited distinction in defining the temporal conjunctions above (Sections 4.1 and 4.2), as certain conjunctions demand an unlimited verb, and others demand a limited verb in one or another of their clauses.

Let's look at the examples. *Until* requires a verb denoting an event of unlimited time span in its main clause, *E1*.

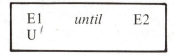

In the first example, the student has used the limited *got* in the main clause. Instead, *was* might be substituted, since it is unlimited.

He was rich until he married.

Similarly, in the second example, *lost* is limited and therefore may not appear in the main clause of an *until* construction. It might be replaced by either of these unlimited verb forms, depending on what the student meant.

My wallet was lost until Juan gave it back.
I didn't have my wallet until Juan gave it back.

After in the third example requires a verb of the limited class in the subordinate clause (E1).

E2   *after*   E1
               L

But *want*, used by the student in his goof, is not a limited verb. Here the student probably meant *decide*, and that is a good substitute since *decide* is limited.

He put on his clean shirt after he decided to go.

In the fourth example, the verb *keep* is unlimited, so it doesn't fit in the E1 clause. One substitute, which is limited and which the student might have meant, is *put*.

After Robert put his coat on the hook, he sat
down to eat.

Of course, one has to learn what students mean to say before substituting verbs that have different meanings. The main thing for the students who make goofs like these to learn is the meaning of the verbs they use, and often the limited-unlimited distinction is part of that meaning. Since the concept limited-unlimited also exists in other languages, it does not have to be taught explicitly. Very often the meaning of temporal conjunctions in other languages also includes these notions. Students must simply learn how English expresses the notions *limited* and *unlimited* by using the proper verbs and verb forms. (See Section 4.10, page 78, for an example of how suitable practice can be given.)

4.5.2 Difficulties in changing limitedness of verbs

Sometimes students make less confusing goofs like these:

†Since the child recovered from measles, he grew well.
†He died until the doctor came.
†They learned French until their tutor quit.
†The ball crashed through the window while
she knitted a sock nearby.

These sound un-English because each conjunction demands an unlimited verb in one of its clauses.

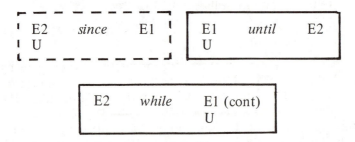

But most inherently limited verbs like those in the goofs can also be interpreted as enduring or continuing for some time when they are in the progressive. And in cases like those, the speaker's intended meaning comes through more clearly if instead of choosing a different, unlimited verb, he uses the original verb in the progressive. The progressive aspect is a regular way of removing the beginning and end points from inherently limited verbs.

> Using the progressive prolongs the action specified by the verb, making the time span unlimited.

So the sentences can be fixed by using the progressive:

Since the child recovered from measles, he has been growing well.
He was dying until the doctor came.
They were learning French until their tutor quit.
The ball crashed through the window while she was knitting a sock nearby.

Some inherently limited verbs which can denote repeated actions like *sneeze, tap,* and *drop*, can be interpreted as unlimited when they appear in E1 clauses with *until* and *while.* In such cases they can be used either in simple tenses or in the progressive. Either way they are interpreted as indicating an indefinitely long series of repetitions of the action. That is why the sentences below are understood as the same in their meanings:

He sneezed until the dust settled.
He was sneezing until the dust settled.

While the mailman tapped on the front door, I went around to the back.
While the mailman was tapping on the front door, I went around to the back.

Such verbs may also be given an unlimited time span by the use of phrases such as *a hundred times, again and again,* or *repeatedly.* Students may produce goofs like the following:

†They were telling us a hundred times.
†She kept her patience while the baby was repeatedly dropping his spoon.
†We listened while the teacher was pronouncing the word again and again.

They need to know that with such phrases, the use of simple tenses is preferred.

They told us a hundred times.

She kept her patience while the baby repeatedly dropped his spoon.
We listened while the teacher pronounced the word again and again.

4.5.3 Misuse of negatives with temporal conjunctions

One other means of making limited verbs unlimited is by using negatives. Even if the verb used in the negative clause is inherently limited, negative clauses are always unlimited. For example, these are unlimited:

He didn't perk up.
That boy hasn't thrown the ball.

Perking up or *throwing a ball* happen instantly, but *not perking up* or *not throwing a ball* drag on endlessly, or until something happens to change matters. Both may therefore be used in the negative state in the E1 of an *until* sentence or the E2 of a *since* sentence.

E1	*until*	E2		E2	*since*	E1
U				U		

He didn't perk up until he smelled the cake baking.
That boy hasn't thrown the ball straight since he joined the team.

This might suggest that E1 with *while* can also take any negative, since E1 with *while* must also be unlimited.

E2 (int)	*while*	E1 (cont)
		U

But *while* differs from *until* and *since* with negatives in its unlimited clause.

†I did it while they didn't look.
†You should practice on your drum while he doesn't study.

Even though E1 is negative, it must be a verb also made

explicitly unlimited by the use of the progressive aspect.

> I did it while they weren't looking.
> You should practice on your drum while he isn't studying.

Students may make goofs in using negatives where a limited verb is required, following *after*

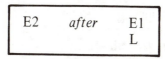

> †After he didn't come, we went looking for him.
> †We had to water the garden after it hadn't rained recently.

These may be corrected by the use of a conjunction such as *when* which can be followed by unlimited verbs.

> When he didn't come, we went looking for him.
> We had to water the garden when it hadn't rained recently.

4.5.4 Misuse of end-of-the-road predicates

The most far-reaching distinction for predicate selection with subordinate conjunctions is verb limitedness. But another interesting semantic distinction comes into play. Think about these goofs:

> †No one should say bad things about him while he is dead.
> †Life is complicated while you are old.
> †We picked these oranges while they were rotten.
> †My nephew was grown up while he was in college.

Compare them with these normal sentences, in which only the adjectives have been changed.

> No one should say bad things about him while he is sick.
> Life is complicated while you are young.
> We picked these oranges while they were green.
> My nephew was growing while he was in college.

In all the normal sentences, *still* can be inserted:

> . . . while he is still sick.
> . . . while you are still young.
> . . . while they were still green.
> My nephew was still growing . . .

But it cannot be added to the other subordinate clauses, even if they are made into main clauses:

> †. . . he is still dead.
> †. . . you are still old.
> †. . . the oranges are still rotten.
> †My nephew was still grown up . . .

Predicates that are compatible with *still* are states that can be expected to give way to other states. *Sickness*, for example, can give way to health, *green* fruit becomes ripe, *young* people become older, etc.

But once something is *rotten, dead, old, demolished,* etc., the further states of progression are not normally considered. Logically, further states may be possible, but this does not affect the selection distinction. After fruit is rotten, it can decay, but relative to being *green*, being *rotten* seems to be the end of the road for its usefulness as edible fruit. So we have characterized this semantic quality as "end-of-the-road."

A few end-of-the-road predicates are:

dead	finished	bald
old	eaten up	grown up
rotten	shattered	mature
demolished	destroyed	adult

While, in addition to selecting unlimited clauses, rules out end-of-the-road predicates in either of its clauses.

E2 (int., not *while*	E1 (cont., not
end-of-the-road)	end-of-the-road)
	U

When may be used instead.

> No one should say bad things about him when he is dead.
> Life is complicated when you are old.
> We picked these oranges when they were rotten.
> My nephew was grown up when he was in college.

Students may also goof in using end-of-the-road predicates in E1 clauses with *until*.

†The fruit had become rotten until we could eat it.
†Everything was eaten up until we came.

```
┌ ─ ─ ─ ─ ─ ─ ─ ─ ─ ─ ─ ─ ─ ─ ┐
│   E1 (not end-of-the-road)      until      E2  │
│   U                                             │
└ ─ ─ ─ ─ ─ ─ ─ ─ ─ ─ ─ ─ ─ ─ ┘
```

Both examples can be fixed by replacing *until* with *before*, since *before* has no end-of-the-road restrictions.

The fruit had become rotten before we could eat it.
Everything was eaten up before we came.

There is an apparent opposite to the end-of-the-road quality which further limits the sentences possible with *until*:

Life is complicated until you are young.
Don't pick the oranges until they are green.

When E2 is a state, *until* means that the beginning of that state marks the end of E1. So if no other state can precede a "beginning-of-the-road" predicate, it cannot fit into the E2 clause after *until*. Some beginning-of-the-road predicates are:

green
young
fresh
new

Goofs with these are most likely to be pure vocabulary errors, *young* being confused with *a young man* or perhaps *a teenager*, and *green* mistaken for *ripe* or *ready*.

Life is complicated until you are a young man.
Don't pick the oranges until they are ripe.

So the definition of *until* can be made more complete:

```
┌─────────────────────────────────────────────┐
│ ⎧  E1 (not          until       E2 (not begin- │
│ ⎨  end-of-the-road)             ing-of-the-road) │
│ ⎩  U                                            │
└─────────────────────────────────────────────┘
```

Suggestions for practice are given in Section 4.11, page 79.

4.6 Superficial tense agreement (STAGR)

4.6.1 Failure to apply STAGR with BEFORE, AFTER, UNTIL, WHILE, WHEN

> †He was rich until he marries.
> †I don't have any money until he gave me some.
> †He wrote the letter after he has found the address.
> †After John drinks the wine, he was sick.

In all these examples, the students have the wrong sequence of tense across clauses. These conjunctions must have the same tense on the first verbal word (auxiliary, *do*, or main verb) in each clause. In the first example, *was* is the first verbal word in the main clause, and *marries* is the first (and only) verbal word in the *until* clause. But *was* is past, and *marries* is present. One correction is to make them both past. Of course, you have to know what the student wants to say.

> He was rich until he married.

The same is true for the other examples. In the second example, *do* is present but *gave* is past. Putting both in the past tense makes the sentence acceptable. *Wrote* and *has* also do not agree in tense, and neither do *drinks* and *was*. Putting these pairs in the past tense corrects the sentences.

> I didn't have any money until he gave me some.
> He wrote the letter after he had found the address.
> After John drank the wine, he was sick.

These goofs all violate a rule called Superficial Tense Agreement (STAGR):

> In both clauses with a temporal conjunction, the first verbal word has the same tense, present or past.[1]

Another rather common type of mistake in tense sequences is to use the present perfect with past tenses. Instead, the simple past or the past perfect should be used,

---

[1]This is a white lie because, with future constructions only the main clause needs to have the future time expressed. This is taken up in Section 4.7, page 77.

depending on the time relationship between the two clauses. For example:

> † When you were here yesterday you have promised to send your picture.
> † After our last pennies have been spent, we wanted to continue our way to Begemdir.
> † My father has lived in Begemdir until he died.
> † The people in the top posts in this world worked until they have reached at their different posts.

For some students, goofs like these may be due to thinking that the present perfect is a past tense. In that case, even if they know that STAGR is required in clauses with certain subordinate conjunctions, these goofs are still likely. They must be shown that the first verbal words are not in the same tense:

> were ≠ have   were = promised
> have ≠ wanted   have = want *or* had = wanted
> has ≠ died   lived = died
> work ≠ have   worked = reached *or* have worked
>   = have reached

Some of the sentences which STAGR allows are not permissible for other reasons of tense usage which students at this level should already be aware of.

> † He has lived in Begemdir until he has died.

When there are two alternate corrections, it is in choosing between them that the student makes the time relationship of the two clauses clear:

> After our last pennies have been spent, we want to continue our way to Begemdir.
> After our last pennies had been spent, we wanted to continue our way to Begemdir.

4.6.2 Inconsistency in perfect use: WHILE

Consider the following examples:

> † While you have worked, I make phone calls.
> † While he has been playing, I am doing all the work.
> † She has been making tea while you are sleeping.

The peculiarity these examples show about *while* concerns aspect sequence: if there is a perfect in E2, there must also be a perfect in E1. Thus, the rule is:

> Use the perfect aspect in both clauses with *while* or in neither.

While you worked, I made a phone call.
While he has been playing. I have done all the work.
She was making tea while you were sleeping.

4.6.3 STAGR misapplied: SINCE

Because there are strict limitations of verb types and tenses with *since* clauses, many mistakes come up:

†I am glad since I came to this   *present in E2*
   country.
†They are studying in this school   *present in both*
   since they are six years old.   *clauses*
†I am studying English since I am   *present in both*
   six, but cannot speak it.   *clauses*
†Since we left in the morning we   *simple past in both*
   only had a liquid food.   *clauses*
†Since he won the lottery, he is   *present in E2*
   happy.

Three of these examples would satisfy STAGR, but they are in fact goofs, as STAGR does not apply with *since*. The rules for tenses with *since* were explained in Section 4.2.6; they may be summarized as:

```
┌ ─ ─ ─ ─ ─ ─ ─ ─ ─ ─ ─ ─ ─ ─ ─ ─ ─ ─ ─ ┐
│  E2                  since   E1          │
│  U (present prefect)         L (simple past)   │
│                              U (present perfect) │
└ ─ ─ ─ ─ ─ ─ ─ ─ ─ ─ ─ ─ ─ ─ ─ ─ ─ ─ ─ ┘
```

This allows the sentences to be formed correctly:

I have been glad since I came to this country.
They have been studying in this school since they were six years old.
I have been studying English since I was six, but I cannot speak it.

Since we left in the morning, we have only had a
liquid food.
Since he won the lottery, he has been happy.

4.7 Superfluous WILL and other future constructions

These local goofs do not interfere much with comprehension, and should be left until more serious mistakes such as clause formation and verb selection have been fixed.

†We will eat after we will pray.
†Before you will leave, you will kiss Grandma.
†I am going to leave here when the new supervisor is going to come.
†We will not eat while he will be standing up.

In all these examples, the subordinate clauses should not have a *will* or the future verb construction in them. They are interpreted as future when the main clause has a *will* or other future in it, so the *will* can be dropped out of the subordinate clause. When that happens, of course, the present tense is put on the remaining verb.

We will eat after we pray.
Before you leave, you will kiss Grandma.
I am going to leave when the new supervisor comes.
We will not eat while he is standing up.

Sentences like these appear as exceptions to STAGR. If letting the student keep a *will* in the subordinate clause helps him learn the general rule of STAGR elsewhere, you may let him keep it there for a while.

PEDAGOGICAL NOTES

4.8 Sentence reordering for conjunction misplacement

Incorrect placement of conjunctions causes major problems for comprehension, so we suggest this be worked on first if it is a problem for your students. It is possible that errors in placement of temporal conjunctions develop from students' feeling that a sentence should never begin with a conjunction, an idea they may have at some point been taught for the coordinate conjunctions *and, or,* and *but.* In that case, they need practice in changing the order of temporal clauses without putting the conjunctions onto the wrong clause. Provide sentences with the conjunction in the middle, and have students switch the two clauses.

> *Cue:*   It was raining when he went out.
> *Response:*When he went out, it was raining.
> *Cue:*   We washed the dishes after we had supper.
> *Response:*After we had supper, we washed the dishes.
> *Cue:*   My brother dropped in while I was visiting my aunt.
> *Response:*While I was visiting my aunt, my brother dropped in.

4.9 Joining finite clauses

Many students say things like this:

> †After leaves . . .
> †While he singing . . .

It helps to have them say two simple sentences which are both finite, and for the teacher to join them with the appropriate conjunction.

> He will leave tonight. We will have dinner.
> After he leaves tonight, we will have dinner.

> It rained. The children went home.
> The children went home before it rained.

After and *before* lend themselves to this exercise most easily, since they connect sequential events. The form of the combined clauses can then be pointed out, and the student can use the conjunctions in his own sentences.

4.10 Diagrams and skits on limited and unlimited verbs

One can show the difference in time span between limited and unlimited verbs diagrammatically, like this:

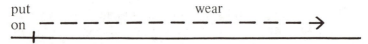

put   wear
on

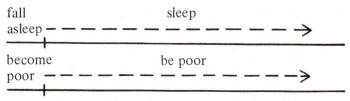

Skits can be used to show the meaning of these. For example, the teacher can have a student put on his coat or his shoes, and while he is going through the necessary motions, tell him that he is *putting* them *on*. Once he has them on, he can no longer put them on; he is now *wearing* them. It may be amusing and effective to show him what it would mean to *put on* his coat all day, or even for fifteen minutes.

Similar activities can be invented for other troublesome limited-unlimited pairs.

4.11 Tables for end-of-the-road predicates

Some end-of-the-road predicates are *old, dead, rotten, finished, demolished, shattered, eaten up,* and *destroyed*. Some beginning-of-the-road adjectives are *green, young, new* and *fresh*. The use of these can be illustrated through a table with *while, until,* and other conjunctions.

	Beginning-of-the-road	Middle-of-the-road	End-of-the-road
	green young	at their peak teen-age middle-aged	rotten old
while until	*yes* *no*	*yes* *yes*	*no* *yes*
when before after	*yes*	*yes*	*yes*

The *yes* and *no* marks indicate the predicates that can appear in the subordinate clause with the temporal conjunction. Of this group, only *while* and *until* are restricted.

Students may be given other beginning- and end-of-the-road predicates and asked both to assign them to the correct columns and to make up sentences using them with appropriate conjunctions.

CHAPTER 5

SENTENTIAL COMPLEMENTS

ANALYSIS OF GOOF TYPES

Subordinate constructions generally take three forms in English: finite clauses, infinitives, and gerunds.[1] One big problem for students is to know when to use infinitives and when gerunds. We will show how this depends on the meaning of the main verb. But first we'll discuss problems students have with the syntax of subordinate constructions. Some kinds of sentential complements have not been included in this chapter. The points we discuss, however, are very basic and should give some insight into the goofs your students make in selecting complement types.

5.1 Misordering in subordinate constructions

†The neighbors say both children he teases.
†He says that he no money has.
†Rufus hopes that is going to U.S.A. soon.
†It is too bad that he coming now.

There are many more examples of this type. The goofs can be avoided by knowing that the only difference between a main clause and a *that*-clause is *that*. And *that* itself can be deleted without making any other change.

> Both main clauses and *that*-clauses have to be finite and they only come in *subject-verb-object* order.[2]

The rule allows the sentences to be corrected:

The neighbors say he teases both children.
He says that he has no money.

---

[1]We do not discuss subjunctives and conditionals here.

[2]The box contains a while lie, since it ignores sentences which are occasional variations on *straight subject-verb-object* sentences, like the emphatic
    Bananas she fixes with onions!
But only main clauses are privileged to do that, never subordinate clauses.

He says that he is going to U.S.A. soon.
It is too bad that he is coming now.

Sometimes students say things like these:

†It is too late milk to buy.
†They are interested in horses riding.
†I want you to see married.
†You will just love Weeki Wachi. I want you to take
there.

In the first two goofs, the verb in the subordinate construction has been put last, just as in the first *that*-clause goof above. The third and fourth goofs have avoided that problem; the students did not say †*I want you married to see* or †*I want you there to take.* Instead they have moved the pronoun object from the subordinate construction to a position after the main verb of the first clause. The rule for them to learn is that:

> The *(subject)-verb-object* order must be kept with infinitives and gerunds.

It is too late to buy milk.
They are interested in riding horses.
I want to see you married.
You will just love Weeki Wachi. I want to take you there.

5.2 Problems with extraposition of fat subject

5.2.1 Omission of surrogate subject

That-clauses in object position, object complements, can be diagrammed like this:

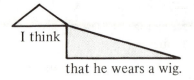

I think
that he wears a wig.

A long or fat constituent like *that he wears a wig* may also show up as the subject of the main clause. These are often called subject complements.

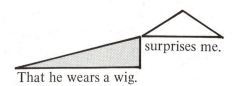

But since English doesn't care for such front-heavy sentences it has a trick for sending the fat constituent to the end, or extraposing it. Students usually sense this and put the fat subject last without prodding, but they often make other goofs in the process. For example:

†Surprises me that he wears a wig.
†Is very hard for me to learn English right.
†Was too bad that the priest could not come.

These are good as far as they go; the student has extraposed the fat subject to the end, an adjustment which is preferred in English and many other languages. But now there's nothing to hold down the front of the sentence where the subject used to be. To compensate, the extraposition rule also insists that the displaced fat subject be replaced by a slim pronoun, *it*, as a surrogate subject.

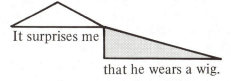

It is very hard for me to learn English right.
It was too bad that the priest could not come.

5.2.2 Wrong surrogate subject: IT and THERE

Sometimes we also hear goofs like these:

†That is funny to see him today.
†That is strange to meet your cousin here.
†He astonishes me that America is so big.
†He is raining today.
†He is warm in here!

The students have to learn that in these cases *it*, and only *it*, can be used as a surrogate subject. This inappropriate use of other pronouns is quite common, especially the use of personal pronouns when describing general conditions like the weather. Students who make these goofs need to learn that the only surrogate subjects are *there* and *it,* and that:

> *It* is used as a surrogate subject when a fat subject has been moved to the end of the sentence, or when weather or other ambient conditions are being described.

It is funny to see him today.
It is strange to meet your cousin here.
It astonishes me that America is so big.
It is raining today.
It is warm in here!

Other students say things like this:

†It was a very tall man here for you.
†It have a dog in here.
†It will be some club meetings on Tuesday.

They need to know that the surrogate subject *there* is used only when the extraposed subject is indefinite (with *a, an some,* a plural noun phrase, or no article at all); the main verb is a form of *be;* and the predicate is a time or place expression, not an adjective or a noun phrase.[1]

> Use of *there* as surrogate subject requires three conditions:
>   (1) extraposed subject is indefinite;
>   (2) verb is *be;*
>   (3) predicate is time or place expression.

Then they can produce the sentences correctly. It may help to set out the components of the sentences in a table, so that the students can see how each of them fulfills a necessary condition for the use of *there.*

---

[1]Occasionally *there* is used without any precise expression of time or place, but this is always in a context where considerations.of time or place are implicit.
    (I looked in his pockets.) There isn't any money.
    (Can we get some ice cream?) No, there's no time (before the bus comes).

main verb BE	*extraposed* *subject* *indefinite*	*predicate* *time or place* *expression*
There was	a very tall man	here for you.
There is	a dog	in here.
There will be	some club meetings	on Tuesday.

It is best to teach the white lie that *there* should be used whenever the conditions in the box are met. This will always give grammatical sentences. As with other white lies, there are other possibilities, but these are more subtle and difficult to learn at first than a set rule which will not lead the student astray.

Some goofs are produced when one of the three conditions given above for *there* is not met:

†There is the library key here.   *subject definite*
†There looked a strange man
   through the window.   *verb not* BE
†There are some elephants very
   ferocious.   *predicate adjective*

These sentences are better left in the standard *subject-predicate* order:

The library key is here.
A strange man looked through the window.
Some elephants are very ferocious.

5.3 Problems with infinitives and gerunds

Infinitives and gerunds are remnants of full clauses. Finite subordinate clauses are reduced to infinitives or gerunds in three cases:

1. When it is unnecessary to mention the subject;
2. When the subject is not nominative; or
3. When the subject of subordinate clause is snatched or moved into the main clause, leaving no subject in the subordinate clause.

5.3.1 Leaving out the subject

The subject of the embedded or subordinate clause can be omitted if it is a repetition of the subject of the first clause. For example:

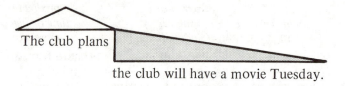

the club will have a movie Tuesday.

Since the second *club* is repetitious, it is omitted. Instead, English speakers say:

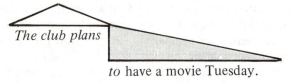

to have a movie Tuesday.

Of course, if the subject of the embedded clause disappears, then the remaining verb is put into its infinitive form, or sometimes into gerund form.

Students sometimes let the subject vanish this way even when it is different from the subject in the main clause. Then they make goofs:

> †I couldn't walk yet after the baby was born, so the doctor didn't want to go home.
> †Daddy has a lot of work. Mother expects to stay at his office late.

Although these are grammatically normal sentences, they do not convey the meanings the speakers intended. Diagrams of their deep structures show what was meant:

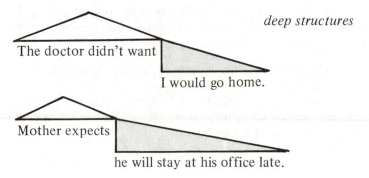

deep structures

The doctor didn't want

I would go home.

Mother expects

he will stay at his office late.

These are not the meanings conveyed by the student sentences above. So to avoid misunderstood sentences, students must learn to apply a rule:

> Only when the subject of an embedded sentence is the same as the subject of the main clause should it be omitted from the subordinate construction.

This is true not only of object complements, but also of subject complements. Here are some goofs illustrating the latter case:

> †I couldn't sleep until you got back. It worries
> me to stay out so late.
> †It astonishes me to be here; I thought you were
> in London.

In both cases, students can be reminded to restore the missing subjects in the appropriate forms:

> I couldn't walk yet after the baby was born,   *infinitives*
> so the doctor didn't want me to go home.
> Daddy has a lot of work. Mother expects him
> to stay at his office late.

> I couldn't sleep until you got back. It   *that-clauses*
> worries me that you stay out so late.
> It astonishes me that you are here; I thought
> you were in London.

A special circumstance must be mentioned regarding the above white lie; we don't have the option of leaving out redundant subjects with all verbs.

> †I think to have my I.D. card in here.
> †Anna told the priest to have six children.

These require a repeated subject:

> I think I have my I.D. card in here.
> Anna told the priest she had six children.

Here is a list of verbs which require the subject to be mentioned even when it is repeated:

think	know	find out	report
tell	notice	say	assume
ignore	doubt	acknowledge	

With some verbs, leaving out the subject should result in

gerunds instead of infinitives. When to choose gerunds or infinitives is discussed at length in Section 5.4, pages 94-98.

From this section, the most important goofs to correct are those like the first ones discussed, which leave out non-repetitious subjects, because with them comprehension troubles set in.

5.3.2 Misformations with non-nominative subjects

Many goofs are made because students misuse a non-nominative subject together with an infinitive or gerund:

> †Him to be so rich is unfair.
> †We plan our class to take a trip.
> †I am sorry for him be disappointed.
>
> †No one regrets them going away.
> †He voting that way was terrible.
> †For me failing the exam would make Mother upset.

Students often don't know that the subject of an infinitive is preceded by *for*, and that the subject of a gerund is in the possessive form. The rule that all these goofs break one way or another is:

```
┌─ ─ ─ ─ ─ ─ ─ ─ ─ ─ ─ ─ ─ ─ ┐
   Non-finite complements look like this:
│                                            │
     subject        predicate
│    For him        to go   infinitive       │
     His            going   gerund
│                                            │
└─ ─ ─ ─ ─ ─ ─ ─ ─ ─ ─ ─ ─ ─ ┘
```

> For him to be so rich is unfair.   *infinitives*
> We plan for our class to take a trip.
> I am sorry for him to be disappointed.
>
> No one regrets their going away.   *gerunds*
> His voting that way was terrible.
> My failing the exam would make Mother upset.

5.3.3 Misformations without subjects

We often see goofs like these:

> †It is necessary for finish the work.
> †It is impossible for to leave right now.

†I will try for drive faster.
†For to catch the bus, go to the next corner.

Goofs like this are very typical and not surprising. The full form of the infinitive with *for* and a subject is presumably the basis of these goofs, as students tend to use no other inappropriate prepositions besides *for*. They can be reminded that an infinitive without a subject is simply preceeded by *to*.

It is necessary to finish the work.
It is impossible to leave right now.
I will try to drive faster.
To catch the bus, go to the next corner.

5.3.4 Special problems with MAKE, LET, HAVE, FIND

It would not do to omit mention of a small but very popular group of main verbs which are exceptions to the rule we have been discussing, as *to* is omitted after them. The three main ones are *make, let, have,* and *find.* Using *to* after such verbs is a fairly minor goof, since it doesn't interfere with comprehension:

†Why won't you let me to go?
†You must have Cielo to bake some delicious bread.

The sentences are corrected very easily:

Why won't you let me go?
You must have Cielo bake some delicious bread.

Make is exceptional in still another way, and we mention it because this construction is so commonly used. When the verb in the complement is *be,* it is left out altogether. *Find* works in the same way.[1]

Students invariably make goofs here:

†Taxes make people to be miserable.
†The doctor can't make her to be thin.
†I just can't make the car to be pretty any more.

With this type of *make* sentence, students must learn the exceptional forms.

---

[1] This construction is also used with *consider,* and by some speakers, particularly British ones, with many more verbs such as *think, believe,* and *know.*

Taxes make people miserable.
The doctor can't make her thin.
I just can't make the car pretty any more.

You may remember that it is not a very important goof to leave out the surrogate subject *it* when a fat subject is extraposed. However, when such a sentence is the object of *make* or *find*, it becomes more important:

†The vacuum cleaner makes easy to clean the house.
†They found pleasant to see you.

When the surrogate subject of *easy* and *pleasant* is restored, the goofs disappear:

The vacuum cleaner makes it easy to clean the house.
They found it pleasant to see you.

Another explanation of such goofs is given in Chapter 6, Section 6.5.3, page 117.

5.3.5 Snatched subject as subject of main clause

Infinitives also show up when the subject of the complement is snatched, or taken to fill the subject position in the main clause. Take the following paraphrases with the main predicate *be likely*:

A. It is likely that the President will be reelected.
B. The President is likely to be reelected.

B is the result of subject snatching. Diagrammatically, this is what happens. Here is the deep structure:

deep structure

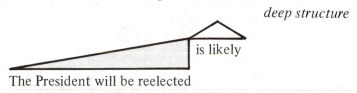

is likely

The President will be reelected

We extrapose the fat subject to the end:

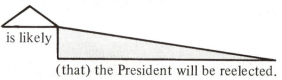

is likely

(that) the President will be reelected.

Now there is a choice. We can insert the surrogate subject *it,* giving:

> *A.* It is likely (that) the President   *surface*
>   will be reelected.   *structure*

Or the subject of the second clause can be snatched to become the subject of the main verb *be likely,* giving:

> *B.* The President is likely to be reelected.   *surface*
>   *structure*

What students don't know is that the second or *B* option, called subject snatching, is open to only a few verbs and adjectives, including:

> appear   seem   turn out
> be likely   be certain be sure

It is also possible with some past participles like:

> said   heard   believed
> rumored   thought

Compare the samples with *be likely* to a pair where the main predicate is *be impossible*:

> *A.* It is impossible that the President will
>   be reelected.
> *B.* †The President is impossible to be reelected.

Students don't know that snatching is as limited as it is, and they overapply it to predicates which look similar or have similar meanings:

> †He is unusual to have a new auto.
> †Volkswagen buses are impossible to go too fast.
> †The door is strange to be unlocked.

With these and others like them, the subject of the subordinate construction must be left there whether it is a *that*-clause or an infinitive. The surrogate subject *it* is employed in either case.

> It is unusual that he has
> a new auto.   *that-clause*
> It is impossible for Volkswagen buses   *infinitive*
> to go too fast.
> It is strange for the door to be unlocked.   *infinitive*

We have to learn for each adjective whether it is allowed to snatch subjects or not. None of the following impersonal adjectives may do so:

possible	necessary	important
impossible	probable	O. K.[1]
strange	difficult	
wonderful	easy	

5.3.6 Snatched subject as object of main clause

Occasionally, we hear sentences like these:

†A girl was decided to play the piano.
†We were demanded to return the hymn book.

This is also a problem of snatching, but in this case, something more complex should be understood. There are verbs which take clauses as objects, but which snatch the subjects of those clauses to make them objects of the main clause. For example, consider this pair of sentences:

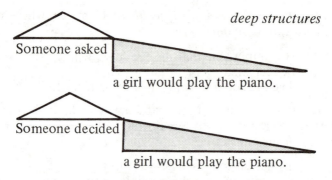

deep structures

Someone asked

a girl would play the piano.

Someone decided

a girl would play the piano.

One of the verbs can snatch *a girl* as its object while the other should not. If the resulting sentences are put into the passive, we have:

A girl was asked to play the piano.   *surface structures*
†A girl was decided to play the piano.

The goof applies a rule for snatching which works with one

---

[1]Further discussion of these and similar adjectives will be found in Chapter 6, Section 6.5, page 115. Most of these "impersonal" adjectives are also used colloquially as responses about people. For example: *How's your boss? Oh, he's just impossible!* Or: *Does the baby give you much trouble? Not at all; he's easy.*

verb, *ask*, to another verb, *decide*. But this must not be done. The subject must remain in the subordinate construction after non-snatching verbs like *decide*:

> It was decided that a girl would play the piano.
> It was demanded that we return the hymn book.

The lesson for students is to know which verbs can snatch like *ask*, and which can't, since otherwise global goofs arise which really affect comprehension.

Snatchers like ASK		*Non-snatchers like* DECIDE	
expect	allow	say	recommend
assume	cause	think	suggest
claim	ask	doubt	demand
permit		hope	

5.3.7 Misformation of gerunds after prepositions

> †We plan on finish this today.
> †My mother believes in to say grace before to eat.
> †I laughed at to hear it.
> †I was delighted at him to resign.

The verbs in these sentences have prepositions tacked on to complete their meanings. Although there· are many such combinations possible in English, all with varying meanings, we will only say this about the form of their verbal complements:

> After prepositions,[1] a complement takes the gerund form or a nominal form.

We plan on finishing this today.
My mother believes in saying grace before eating.
I laughed at hearing it.
I was delighted at his resignation.

Verb and *to* combinations are especially troublesome:

> †I am *used to* go without breakfast.
> †His behavior will *lead to* go to prison.
> †We *look forward to* see you again.

---

[1]*To,* when used as an infinitive attacher, is not considered a preposition.

The *to's* here belong to the first verb, in that they are necessary to complete their meaning and so should be followed by gerunds instead of infinitives. They are not plain infinitive attachers, as these students may think.

A simple test to help students tell whether *to* is a meaning completer or an infinitive attacher is this: replace the complement with a noun object and see whether the *to* still belongs there:

> †I am used breakfast.
> I am used to breakfast.

If *to* must be present, as here, then it is a meaning completer and a verb in the complement must be a gerund:

> I am used to going without breakfast.
> His behavior will lead to going to prison.
> We look forward to seeing you again.

When your advanced students begin using verbs that have a negative meaning, such as *prevent, keep, prohibit, stop, dissuade* and *discourage*, they should learn that the only appropriate preposition to follow them is *from*.

> †I prevented him to going with me.
> †We kept him for to see her.

They must become familiar with the use of *from*:

> I prevented him from going with me.
> We kept him from seeing her.

When they do learn to use *from* with these verbs, another goof often crops up:

> †I cannot prevent you from to do that, but I'm not responsible.
> †You must not discourage him from to write what he must.
> †Why do you prohibit your sister from to kiss me?

The rule for these is same as above: after prepositions, verbs must appear in their gerund form.

> I cannot prevent you from doing that, but I'm not responsible.
> You must not discourage him from writing what he must.
> Why do you prohibit your sister from kissing me?

5.4 Choosing complement types by main verb meaning

We have discussed a number of goofs in this chapter that have to do with the form of complements. You can see that these goofs can be mechanically corrected by observing the rules for complement formation.

However, there is another, more pervasive question: how can we tell which form of complement is appropriate for any given verb? Which verbs take finite clauses after them, and which verbs take infinitives? When do gerunds appear? Many of these questions can be answered by meaning, so we will organize the complement system according to the meaning of the main verb.

5.4.1 Forms taken by propositions and actions

†Mark thinks the beans needing fertilizer.
†He resented that I went.
†We will want that he visits us.

Constructions following main verbs of mental action like *believe, claim, think,* and *regret* may be judged as true or false. Such statements, or propositions, can all be represented by finite *that*-clauses, though they may also be represented by constructions derived from *that*-clauses.[1] Constructions which follow certain adjectives such as *true, false, likely,* and *obvious* are also construed as propositions. Here are some examples:

Mark thinks that the beans need fertilizer.	*that-clauses*
It is obvious that time is on our side.	
We believed him to own the ranch. (= that he owned the ranch.)	*infinitive = that-clause*
I regretted his having insulted her. (= that he had insulted her.)	*gerund = that-clause*

On the other hand, constructions which follow main verbs like *want, force, stop* and *prevent* do not invite judgment as true or false. They are construed as simply describing events, or actions. Typically these constructions do not appear in *that*-clause form, but are only gerunds or infinitives.

---

[1] A few verbs of mental action such as *know* and *think* do not usually take infinitives.

He resented my going.   *gerund*
We will want him to visit us.   *infinitive*
The choir stopped singing.   *gerund*
He didn't force anyone to cooperate.   *infinitive*

5.4.2 Difficulty with verbs which select infinitives

†Why did you tell them not looking at each other?
†Nobody wants doing that.
†I don't expect seeing him today.
†We will offer carrying the furniture.
†Remember putting out the trash tomorrow.

Typically, the action described in an infinitive complement takes place later than the process described by the main verb. Perhaps this can be seen best with a verb that also takes a proposition as a complement:

He has decided that he will go.   *that-clause*
He has decided to go.   *infinitive*

Decide to go clearly means that the *deciding* took place before the action that will follow, *going*. And this is why the future *will* can be deleted from the subordinate structure when the infinitive is formed. The meaning of *decide to go* includes the idea that the *going* is still a prospective action. Thus to have the future tense expressed in the subordinate construction with the infinitive would just be redundant.

Main verbs which take action complements often have infinitives as complements. In the goofs above, infinitives should have been used instead of gerunds, as the action described in the complement is prospective in each case.

Why did you tell them not to look at each other?
Nobody wants to do that.
I don't expect to see him today.
We will offer to carry the furniture.
Remember to put out the trash tomorrow .

Here is a list of some main verbs which can normally take infinitive complements:

that-clauses and infinitives

decide	tell	intend	promise	persuade
expect	request	plan	hope	threaten

infinitives

want	help	forbid	strive
order	aid	allow	attempt
force	assist	encourage	refuse
offer	try	choose	

5.4.3 Difficulty with verbs which select gerunds

†I resent Tom to come home so late.
†Don't you remember to see her yesterday?
†Most of the pupils enjoy to have a holiday.
†Let's ignore him to bother us.

Main verbs whose usual complements are gerunds are most often those whose meaning implies that the action described by the gerund has already taken place. The main verb expresses a reaction to the accomplished fact. Or, if the gerund represents a proposition, it is presumed to be true, as in *People resent their having overlooked the groom's father.* In fact:

> Any time you can say *the fact that* followed by a sentence, the whole phrase can be replaced by the gerund form.

Thus, these two phrases are equivalent:

The fact that he is here = his being here.

It wouldn't hurt to teach the white lie that:

> Verbs which can put *the fact* before their *that*-clause complements do not snatch subjects or take infinitives.

Again the meaning can be seen most clearly with a verb that takes both kinds of complements.

He regrets that he hurt his friend.   *that-clause*
He regrets hurting his friend.   *gerund*

To regret hurting someone means the hurting has already been done. This meaning can be seen in the *that*-clause which is in the past tense, and is implicit in gerunds when they occur in action complements as well.

With this knowledge, the goofs above are easily explained. The students have used an infinitive when the meaning of the main verb was that the action described in the complement was done already. Gerunds should have been used:

I resent Tom's coming home so late.
Don't you remember seeing her yesterday?
Most of the pupils enjoy having a holiday.
Let's ignore his bothering us.

Here is a list of some main verbs which normally can take gerund complements:[1]

that-clauses and gerunds		gerunds
regret	admit	finish
ignore	appreciate	stop
resent	acknowledge	prevent (from)
notice	remember	enjoy
reveal	recall	

The examples with *remember* in this and the preceding section illustrate the semantic difference between gerunds and infinitives clearly. *Remember* has two meanings, and each meaning demands one complement type. It can describe a memory of a past experience:

Don't you remember seeing her   *gerund*
yesterday?

Or it can describe a future task which is still prospective:

Remember to put out the trash   *infinitive*
tomorrow.

Forget is similar.[1] It can refer to a past event or to a future one depending on whether a gerund or an infinitive is used:

He forgot telling her the rumor.   *gerund*
He forgot to tell her the rumor.   *infinitive*

---

[1] The *accomplished-fact* meaning is not generally present when a complement must be a gerund simply because it follows a preposition, as after *prevent from*.

[2] A few verbs take either gerunds or infinitives without much change in meaning. *Begin, start, try,* and *like* are some of these. *I like to read* and *I like reading* are virtually identical. Some adjectives in impersonal constructions have the same flexibility; for instance, *It's nice to see you again* and *It's nice seeing you again*. Subject complements which aren't extraposed can take either form: for instance, *Their forgetting it annoyed us,* or *For them to forget it annoyed us*.

5.4.4 Confusion over complement form after auxiliaries

†I will enjoy to swim.
†They had hoped going, but couldn't.

It should be noted that:

> The use of auxiliaries does not change the selection of complement forms.

Students should learn that *enjoy* takes a gerund since we usually know what we enjoy only after we have done it. Similarly, what we *hope* for is a prospect and gets expressed by an infinitive. The auxiliaries don't change these semantic characteristics of the main verbs, and so don't change the form of their complements.

I will enjoy swimming.
They had hoped to go, but couldn't.

PEDAGOGICAL NOTES

5.5 Combining clauses with THAT

To help students learn that *that*-clauses are finite, give them two full sentences of which one can be subordinate to the other and have them insert *that*. Tell them that all *that*-clauses are full sentences, with a nominative subject and a verb which agrees with the subject.

Cue: The world is round. Columbus knew it.
Response: Columbus knew that the world is round.

The same kind of exercise can be used to show that the word order in subordinate clauses is the same as in main clauses: *subject-verb-object*.

5.6 Drilling IT and THERE

Leaving out the surrogate subject *it* is a problem that seems almost impossible to overcome, since students know that they can be understood whether it is present or not. We can only suggest drilling home, time and time again, that English sentences must have something in subject position and the only surrogate subjects are *there* and *it*.

If your students confuse *there* and *it*, we suggest teaching them the limited conditions under which *there* can be used as a subject. (See Section 5.2.2, page 83.) Then you can give them sample sentences to transform with *there* only if they are suitable.

Cue:	A new visitor was here today.
Response:	There was a new visitor here today.
Cue:	Snow fell onto the house. *verb not* BE
Response:	Snow fell onto the house.
Cue:	Some snow was on the house.
Response:	There was some snow on the house.

Similar work can be done with *it* when the rules for its use are known. (See Section 5.2.2, page 83.) Students should remember that surrogate subjects have no preceding reference, and realize that you are not talking about sentences where *it* refers to a noun in the preceding sentence, like:

I wrote the letter. It was lost in the mail.

5.7 TO and FOR with infinitives

Unfortunately, our only suggestion is that students who put wrong prepositions before infinitives must remember that only *to* appears, and no other. (See Section 5.3.7, page 92.) And if the subject of an infinitive is present, they need to remember that *for* precedes that subject. (See Section 5.3.2, page 87.) It may be useful to drill these rules using sentences that begin with *it* and *there*:

It is important for you to hurry up!
It is astounding for him to be here.
It is necessary to talk clearly.
There is time for us to eat before we go.

5.8 Making a verb and complement table

You can help advanced students see the semantic difference between gerunds and infinitives by leading them to induce it for themselves. A strategy for doing this is to have the class make up a chart showing, for a number of verbs which take propositions as complements, whether each takes a gerund or infinitive construction, and what the tense is in the corresponding *that*-clause.

You could, of course, just give them the relevant examples, but it gives the students more practice, and more to think about, if they provide the examples themselves. It should be made clear to them that there is no penalty for mistakes; they should be encouraged to say things they're not sure of. A lesson in which this is done might go like this:

> *Teacher:* Can you use *hope* in a sentence?
> *Student:* I hope to get a raise.
> *Teacher:* *(writing the answer on the board)* Can you say that another way, with *that*?
> *Student:* I hope that I will get a raise.

Do this for lots of verbs that take prospective actions as complements: for instance, *decide, plan, intend, expect,* and *promise.* Write each elicited pair of sentences on the board and underline the complements.

Then start a summary chart:

verb	that-clause	infinitive
hope	✓	✓
decide	✓	✓
plan	✓	✓

Ask the class:

> *Teacher:* Do we have *that* clauses with *decide*?
> Do we have infinitives with *decide*?

Put checks in the appropriate columns when the students answer *yes*. Do this for all the verbs the students have been using in sentences.

Then switch to consideration of gerunds.

> *Teacher:* We have been talking about sentences getting reduced so they come out as infinitives, with *to* before the verb. How else can sentences be reduced?
> *Student:* With *ING* or with gerunds.

Ask students to use verbs that take propositions with accomplished facts as complements, for instance *regret, resent, ignore,* and *notice.* Elicit both *that*-clauses and the gerund forms.

> *Student:* He regrets that he came. He regrets coming.

Add a column for *gerunds* to the chart and mark it appropriately for each verb taking a gerund.

verb	that-clause	infinitive	gerund
hope	✓	✓	
decide	✓	✓	
plan	✓	✓	
regret	✓		✓
resent	✓		✓

Now ask, if the matter has not yet come up:

> *Teacher:* How would it sound to use an infinitive with *regret? I regret him to come.* Is that an English sentence?
>
> *Student:* No, it isn't.
>
> *Teacher:* What would it sound like to use a gerund with *hope?*
>
> *Student:* *I hope getting a raise.* That isn't English either.

Many teachers might balk at allowing and even encouraging students to come up with ungrammatical sentences. However, it is important for advanced students to develop an ear for what is grammatical in English, so that it becomes second nature. This type of question helps to achieve this aim as well as to get across the particular point at hand. Continue until it is clear that each verb on the chart takes either a gerund or an infinitive construction in place of a *that*-clause.

Now you have elicited a chart that should make it easy for students to see what it is about a verb that makes it select an infinitive or a gerund. Ask them to compare all the *that*-clauses that correspond to infinitives and those that correspond to gerunds. They do not usually have trouble seeing that there's a future *will* in all *that*-clauses corresponding to infinitives, and a past tense in *that*-clauses corresponding to gerunds.

It's then easy to extend this distinction to verbs which take not *that*-clauses but actions, like *force, want, encourage* and *offer* on one hand, and *finish, enjoy,* and *stop* on the other. Let students give you examples with such verbs:

> *Student:* Let's offer to help at the sale.
> Do you enjoy swimming?
> The mechanic finished fixing the car.

5.9 Choice between gerund and infinitive with REMEMBER, FORGET and STOP

There are some especially troublesome verbs: *stop, remember,* and *forget.* Sentences like these are all too common:

> †When his brother got lung cancer, he stopped to smoke.
> †I remember to meet you at the party last night.

These are really confusing, and hard for students to get straight because the verbs take both gerunds and infinitives, but each construction has a different meaning. So to use the wrong one also gives the wrong meaning.

However, the different meanings can be explained by what the students have already figured out about gerunds and infinitives: that gerunds are used with accomplished facts and infinitives with prospective actions. When you *remember to do* something, the doing follows the remembering. But *to remember doing* something, you are thinking back about the event which has already happened.

Goofs with *stop* can also be explained this way: *to stop to smoke* means to stop doing something else *in order to* smoke. Clearly, at the time you stop, the thing you were doing is an accomplished fact while the smoking is prospective. On the other hand, when you stop smoking, smoking is in your past, accomplished and presumably done with.

5.10 Headline decipherment

Subject-snatching constructions, especially passive ones, are often found in headlines:

headline	*full sentence*
TWO MORE JAPANESE EX-SOLDIERS REPORTED SIGHTED ON GUAM	Two more Japanese ex-soldiers *have been* reported sighted on Guam.
ACCORD SAID TO BE NEAR	An accord *is* said to be near.

Students who readily understand such headlines will not have trouble completing them. One way to practice working with verbs which snatch subjects is to ask students to make impersonal constructions from them with *that*-clauses:

It is reported that two ex-soldiers have been sighted on Guam.

It is _____ that _____ .

It is said that an accord is near.

It is _____ that _____.

Students can be encouraged to watch for headlines in the newspapers which display similar structures. These can serve as a useful source for further practice of impersonal constructions, as well as giving review of the auxiliaries and articles which are so frequently omitted.

CHAPTER 6

PSYCHOLOGICAL PREDICATES

DEFINITIONS

6.1 Straightforward and reverse verbs

Many predicates, both verbs and adjectives, describe psychological states or reactions. They tell how a person feels about something or someone. Two things are implicit in the meaning of such verbs: a person who experiences the feeling, called the experiencer, and the thing or person that stimulates the feeling, the stimulus.

6.1.1 Straightforward psychological verbs

Most verbs that can relate an animate noun (one that can do or experience things, a living being) and an inanimate noun make it come out so that the animate one is the subject and the inanimate one the object.

For example, we say:

John ate	the chocolates.
The man repaired	typewriters.

But we don't say:

*The chocolates ate John.
*Typewriters repaired the man.

Some psychological verbs act just like ordinary verbs; the subject is the experiencer and the object is the stimulus. For example:

experiencer	*stimulus*
He loves	that color.
We can't stand	chocolates.

The subject *he* is experiencing the feeling of loving, and *that color* is what stimulates the feeling. We won't pay much attention to sentences with straightforward predicates like these because students rarely have any problems with them, unless they confuse them with reverse predicates. (See Section 6.2.2, page 108.) So straightforward psychological verbs like *love, enjoy*, etc. are just like *eat* and *repair*. That is, we say:

experiencer	stimulus
John loved	the chocolates.
He enjoyed	them.

But we don't say:

*The chocolates loved John.
*They enjoyed him.
    The rule here is that

> With straightforward psychological verbs, the word order is *experiencer-verb-stimulus*.

Here is a partial list of straightforward psychological verbs:

love	admire	hate	regret
like	respect	fear	mistrust
enjoy	prefer	dread	trust
remember	not mind	dislike	understand
miss	forget	resent	not be able to stand

6.1.2 Reverse psychological verbs

There is also a group of psychological predicates where the order of animate and inanimate is the other way around. These are called reverse psychological verbs. With reverse verbs, the stimulus, which is typically but not necessarily inanimate,[1] shows up as the subject, while the experiencer, which must be animate, is the object.

> With reverse psychological verbs, the word order is *stimulus-verb-experiencer*.

A comparison of these verbs with *eat* and *like* makes the distinction clear.

---

[1] The stimulus can be animate too:
    The baby amuses us.
    Joshua delighted the children with his antics.

John ate the chocolates.   *ordinary verb*
John liked the chocolates.   *straightforward psychological verb*

The chocolates pleased John.   *reverse psychological verb*

But not:

   *John pleased the chocolates.

The reverse verbs cause all the trouble because students have no way of knowing, just by looking at one, that it is reverse. There is no apparent reason why two almost synonymous sentences like these do not have their subjects and objects the other way around:

   I don't mind that.   *straightforward verb*
   That doesn't bother me.   *reverse verb*

We cannot say:

   *That doesn't mind me.
   *I don't bother that.

Here are some of the reverse psychological verbs:

delight	surprise	bother	disgust
thrill	interest	worry	shock
charm	fascinate	disappoint	scare
amuse	satisfy	depress	frighten
excite	relieve	annoy	horrify
elate	reassure	bore	appall
impress	overwhelm	confuse	insult
please	flatter	mislead	offend

ANALYSIS OF GOOF TYPES

6.2 Misordering of subject and object

6.2.1 Misordering with reverse psychological verbs

Here are some typical goofs with reverse verbs:

   †The cat is on the dinner table, but my father doesn't bother that.
   †I have impressed Plato.

†Do you surprise me?
†Call your mother; she worries you.

These students have failed to reverse the order of experiencer and stimulus, as these verbs require, so now the meanings are confused. The first two don't make sense, and in the second two it is not clear who is surprising or worrying whom. Students must remember the rule of *stimulus-verb-experiencer* word order and learn the group of reverse verbs given in Section 6.1.2 above.

The cat is on the dinner table, but that doesn't bother my father.
Plato has impressed me.
Do I surprise you?
Call your mother; you worry her.

Errors like this with the wrong order of elements are the basis of all the other problems with reverse verbs. This is an important reason for giving these goofs priority in the hierarchy. Until the basic order is corrected, the whole structure is rotten at the base; the elements are playing the wrong syntactic roles. That is why these global misordering goofs are important to correct early.

6.2.2 Misordering with straightforward psychological verbs

When students are learning the rule about word order with reverse psychological verbs, they often overapply it to straightforward verbs as well:

†And physical geography prefer me more than anything else.
†The party enjoyed Aziz.
†Do I love you? Tell me yes.

These are confusing because the grammatical relations are garbled. The roles of experiencer and stimulus have been exchanged. Since these are straightforward verbs, the word order should be *experiencer-verb-stimulus*.

I prefer physical geography more than anything else.
Aziz enjoyed the party.
Do you love me? Tell me yes.

Students need to remember that these pattern normally.

6.3 Embedded sentences with reverse verbs

The reverse verbs present an extra difficulty when they appear in complex sentences, that is, sentences which have an embedded clause. There are several common paraphrases used by English speakers:

> It surprised Mary that he came so late.
> Mary was surprised that he came so late.
> It was surprising to Mary that he came so late.

6.3.1 Using the experiencer as subject

Here are goofs students make with these types of sentences:

> †I surprise that he likes it.
> †I delight that you are so thin.
> †His parents annoy that he always goes to the cinema.

They must learn that with reverse verbs:

> The experiencer can become the subject only if the reverse verb is changed into the participial form with *ED*.

And of course *be* must precede this form of a verb. This means the following corrections can be made:

experiencer		*stimulus*
I	am surprised	that he likes it.
I	am delighted	that you are so thin.
His parents	are annoyed	that he always goes to the cinema.

Alternatively, students who don't want to put the stimulus before the verb can be shown how to extrapose the stimulus by using a surrogate subject, as discussed below in Section 6.3.5, page 111.

6.3.2 Wrong use of prepositions with ED forms

> †We were all bored about his teaching.

Whenever *ED* is added to reverse verbs, particular prepositions may follow. These prepositions differ from verb to verb. For example, we say:

interested in	*but rarely*	*depressed in
confused about	*but rarely*	*bored about
annoyed at	*but rarely*	*satisfied at
overwhelmed with	*but rarely*	*excited with

These are typical goofs and seem to persist despite a teacher's efforts. We suggest that since *by* is most commonly used, it may be less painful to allow its use after all these verbs.

We were all bored by his teaching.

It is true that the different prepositions vary in meaning, but when students misuse them, comprehension is usually not much interfered with, and especially not if they use *by*. However, for advanced students who want to learn the finer subtleties of English, precise use of prepositions is essential. If their problems seem to persist, remember that even native speakers of English take a long time to learn these subtle distinctions.

6.3.3 Confusing ED and ING forms of reverse verbs

Another type of goof that commonly comes up is this:

†I was surprising that he came.
†I was boring with his speech.
†Tell me what you are disgusting by.
†He is so interesting in business.

Almost all reverse verbs can be made into adjectival forms by adding *ING*. But unlike the *ED* forms, the *ING* ones cannot modify the experiencer. Instead, they modify the stimulus, whether in a simple or in a complex sentence.

I was surprised by the weather.
The weather was surprising (to me).
I was pleased that he came.
It was pleasing (to me) that he came.

So students who make goofs like those above must learn:

> *ING* forms of reverse verbs take the stimulus as subject. *ED* forms take the experiencer as subject.

The goofs could be corrected by maintaining the word order and changing the verb to the *ED* form:

I was surprised that he came.
I was bored with his speech.
Tell me what you are disgusted by.
He is so interested in business.

Or they could be corrected by retaining the *ING* form of the verb and changing the word order:

It was surprising (to me) that he came.
His speech was boring (to me).
Tell me what is disgusting to you.
Business is so interesting to him.

Note that if the experiencer is mentioned, it must be preceded by a preposition, usually *to*.

Adding *ING* to psychological verbs is a fairly general way of making adjectival forms. But for some of these verbs, special suffixes are added instead:

bother	bothersome
please	pleasant
delight	delightful
impress	impressive
scare	scary

And for a few, a derived noun is used instead of an adjective:

relieve	a relief

These forms must simply be memorized.

For psychological verbs which consist of a verb and a particle, such as *mix up, bowl over, turn on/off,* or *set back,* there is no *ING* form.

6.3.4 Leaving out stimulus or experiencer

Reverse psychological verbs are transitive, so we can't use them in the active form without mentioning both a stimulus and an experiencer. But sometimes this is not desirable. A reasonable attempt to omit one or the other can lead to grammatical goofs:

†Don't go to that movie. It bores.
†When Judge Fielding takes his cloak off, he doesn't impress very much.

†When Americans excite, they talk too fast for me.
†Why did you depress yesterday?

In the first two sentences there is no reason to mention who feels *bored* or *impressed*; the students are trying to express objective judgments about the movie and the judge. They are trying to avoid naming the experiencer. What they are looking for are adjectives which modify the stimulus, that is, the *ING* forms and related adjectives.

Don't go to that movie. It's boring.
When Judge Fielding takes his cloak off, he isn't very impressive.

In the second pair of goofs, the students are talking about feelings of *excitement* and *depression* without specific or known stimuli. They may know well enough that these verbs take the experiencer as object, but there is nothing else around to be the subject. They need adjectives which modify the experiencer, *ED* forms.

When Americans are excited, they talk too fast for me.
Why were you depressed yesterday?

6.3.5 Mismanaged extraposition

What happens with reverse verbs when the stimulus is particularly long, or fat? The nature of reverse verbs would allow any stimulus to show up in first place, even fat ones like these:

That he buried the money under the tree reassures us.
That the cat is on the kitchen table bothers him.

But fat constituents don't appear first too often, because to most of us they sound awkward. And students have the same preference, even if it means making other mistakes:

†Everyone delights that you won the lottery.
†Sarah annoys that the ice cream is so soft.
†I bore that we always have to study.

You already know that putting the fat stimulus last can be accomplished by using the *ED* form of reverse verbs. This gives:

Everyone is delighted that you won the lottery.

Sarah is annoyed that the ice cream is so soft.
I am bored that we always have to study.

Another way to fix these goofs is with extraposition[1] where the surrogate subject *it* is inserted in the subject position and the fat clause is moved to the end of the sentence.

surrogate subject	*experiencer*	*stimulus*
It delights	everyone	that you won the lottery.
It annoys	Sarah	that the ice cream is so soft.
It bores	me	that we always have to study.

In this case, the *ED* form of the reverse verb may not be used. But extraposition does work with the *ING* form of the verb, if the experiencer is omitted or preceded by *to*.

surrogate subject	*experiencer*	*stimulus*
It is delightful	to everyone	that you won the lottery.
It is annoying	to Sarah	that the ice cream is so soft.
It is boring		that we always have to study.

Any one of the three types of corrections will give good English. After students know one form, such as the *ED* sentences, they can begin to learn the other paraphrases.

Sometimes when students are still mixing up the order of elements with reverse verbs, they produce goofs with both short, or slim, and fat stimuli:

†He doesn't scare snakes.
†He doesn't bother that you are so late today.

For comprehension, the second is much more innocuous than the first, though syntactically they are exactly the same. The main reason the misplaced slim stimulus makes more trouble

---

[1]Extraposition is discussed in Chapter 5, Section 5.2.1, page 81.

is that the resulting sentence is more likely to be ambiguous, especially when the stimulus is animate, as above.

But even though the slim stimulus causes greater comprehension problems, we urge you to pay equal attention to both if the student says both, because not to do so would obscure the fact that they are the same problem. Slim or fat, a stimulus is a stimulus and must be the subject of a reverse verb, unless extraposition is used.

> Snakes don't scare him.
> It doesn't bother him that you are so late today.

All your work in teaching reverse verbs will come to nothing if the student learns to correct the order only with some stimuli and not with all of them.

This is a clear case where the hierarchy of comprehension difficulty is not enough to dictate pedagogical order. In this case, it is better to be systematic in enforcing the rules even if goofs like the second do not seem very serious.

6.4 Straightforward adjectives

Adjectives which describe psychological states or reactions may also be straightforward or reverse.

> With straightforward psychological adjectives, the word order is *experiencer-verb-adjective*.

Here is a list of some straightforward adjectives:

glad	fortunate	angry	sorry
happy	lucky	furious	sad
eager	reluctant	mad	afraid
crazy about	impatient	anxious	

6.4.1 Misordering with straightforward adjectives

Students sometimes treat straightforward adjectives as if they were reverse. They use the stimulus, instead of the experiencer, as subject, and make goofs like these:

> †It was impatient to me to find out my grade.
> †The broken vase was furious to the shopkeeper.
> †Going home alone is afraid.

They need to learn that straightforward adjectives are used just like the *ED* participial forms of reverse verbs; the experiencer is the subject, and the stimulus need not be mentioned. And understanding this, they have to learn which adjectives are straightforward.

The goofs should be corrected so the experiencer is the subject:

> I was impatient to find out my grade.
> The shopkeeper was furious about the broken vase.
> I am afraid to go home alone.

In the last example, if the student doesn't mean *I am afraid* but *anybody would be afraid*, a reverse adjective like *frightening* can be substituted for *afraid*.

> Going home alone is frightening.

When the stimulus is a noun phrase, as in the second example, it must be attached by a preposition. Though it is not always correct, *about* is the most generally usable one with straightforward adjectives.

6.4.2 Misuse of adjectives as verbs

Sometimes students think some of these adjectives are verbs:

> †Kwame sorries so much that your wife is sick.
> †We lucky that we met.

They need to learn that straightforward psychological adjectives, like all adjectives, can only appear after *be* or *become*, or a few other verbs like *feel* and *seem*. Possible corrections for these goofs are:

> Kwame is sorry so much that your wife is sick.
> We are lucky that we met.

Occasionally both misordering and misuse as a verb are piled into a single sentence with a straightforward adjective:

> †It sads me in my heart to leave you.
> †It happied my mother that I was passing my course.

The two corrections must be combined to give good sentences:

I am sad in my heart to leave you.
My mother was happy that I was passing my course.

6.5 Reverse adjectives

So far all the reverse predicates we have discussed have been verbs. There are also adjectives which take the stimulus as subject, just like adjectives derived from reverse verbs by *ING* and other suffixes. Here are some reverse adjectives:

good	possible	difficult	stupid
wonderful	impossible	hard	bad
important	probable	terrible	sad[1]
necessary	fantastic	awful	fortunate[1]
easy	strange	painful	lucky[1]
O. K.	great	simple	

Both types of reverse adjectives pattern alike, that is, take the same order of constituents:

His idea is wonderful.   *reverse adjectives*
Their behavior is terrible.

Their idea is exciting.   *ING form of reverse*
Their behavior is annoying.   *verbs*

The plain reverse adjectives do not always include the experiencer as readily as the derived *ING* adjectives.

†His idea is wonderful to me. *reverse adjective*
His idea is surprising to me. *ING form of reverse*
                                               verb

6.5.1 Misordering with reverse adjectives

Sometimes students treat reverse adjectives as though they were straightforward, and put an experiencer instead of a stimulus in subject position, even with those adjectives like *wonderful* which prefer not to have an experiencer directly attached.

†I am hard to get anything done.
†He is easy learning mechanical things.
†You are important to come on time.

---

[1]You will notice that a few adjectives can be used either as straightforward or as reverse.

†Talmy was painful that his mother was crying.
†The principal is O. K. that you borrowed this.
†I am wonderful to see you.

In every sentence, the stimulus must appear first, since:

> Reverse adjectives take the stimulus as subject. The word order is *stimulus-verb-adjective*.

The correction we suggest is to use the surrogate subject *it*:

It is hard for me to get anything done.
It is easy for him to learn mechanical things.
It is important for you to come on time.
It was painful for Talmy that his mother was crying.
It is O.K. (with the principal) that you borrowed this.
It is wonderful to see you.

6.5.2 Misordering in embedded sentences

Goofs like those above are often the basis for worse ones when the sentences are embedded:

†He admits me hard to learn quickly.
†He thinks you important to hurry up.

Here the main clauses are:

He admits . . .
He thinks . . .

The mistakes are in the embedded sentences, which are:

†I am hard to learn quickly.
†You are important to hurry up.

These should be corrected to:

It is hard for me to learn quickly.
It is important for you to hurry up.

The subordinate clauses can now be embedded as simple *that*-clauses, and we have:

He admits (that) it is hard for me to learn quickly.
He thinks (that) it is important for you to hurry up.

Because the simple embedded clauses were wrong, so were

the whole sentences in the student examples.

In many cases with straightforward personal adjectives, the result of embedding is fine. Students tend to be more familiar with and speak more correctly with straightforward personal predicates like *happy* and *angry*. They are less familiar with the impersonal reverse adjectives like *easy, hard* and *important*, and so tend to goof more frequently with them.

6.5.3 Difficulties with causation

Sometimes goofs like this occur:

> †The kids *make impossible* me to work.
> †She *finds easy* to *make delicious* the food.

Superficially, one can correct the first one by simply inserting *it* before *impossible*, and *for* after it. In the second, one can insert *it* before *easy* and *the food* before *delicious*.

But it may be that for many students the italicized words seem to form a single, complex verb. For example, English has the causative verb:

> He saddens me.

However, English has another, more general alternative, using *make*:

> He makes me sad.

And this is the construction students have to learn.[1]

Students whose languages only express causation by putting an affix on a word, as English occasionally does with *EN (sadden)* or *IFY (beautify)* will make mistakes of this sort most often, since *make* serves the same purpose as an affix of causation in their language. Once they see how *make* works, the corrections will be understood, not just memorized as isolated sentences.

> The kids make it impossible for me to work.
> She finds it easy to make the food delicious.

Students who have difficulty with *make* maybe encouraged to watch for such constructions in their reading, and in particular to note the use of *it* with impersonal adjectives such as *impossible, easy*, or *necessary*.

---

[1]*Make* and the need to have an object preceding its adjective *(make me sad)* is discussed in Chapter 5, Section 5.3.4, page 88.

PEDAGOGICAL NOTES

Perhaps the most productive way to help students learn how to use reverse psychological verbs is to wait until they use one wrong. (You won't have to wait long.) At that time, exercises and practice will be most beneficial.

6.6 Word order exercises

6.6.1 Scrambling and substitution

If word order with reverse psychological verbs is a problem, give students pairs of sentences with straightforward and reverse verbs, scrambled.

reverse	*straightforward*
disgust chocolates thin people	love chocolates fat people

When the sentences are properly unscrambled, try substitution drills, using as cues verbs, experiencers and stimuli. For instance, remove both verbs from the above sentences and then give the class verbs to insert in the proper one.

Cue:	Enjoy.
Response:	Fat people enjoy chocolates.
Cue:	Hate.
Response:	Fat people hate chocolates.
Cue:	Thin people.
Response:	Thin people hate chocolates.
Cue:	Please.
Response:	Chocolates please thin people.
Cue:	Appreciate
Response:	Thin people appreciate chocolates.
Cue:	Delight (etc.)

Whenever possible, start such a drill with a sentence said by one of the students, and try to end up with the same one so as to make the break in the conversation more meaningful. Once the patterning, the order of experiencer and stimulus, is understood with both types of verb, the students should learn the group of reverse verbs. (See Section 6.1.2, page 106 for a list.) The straightforward psychological verbs pattern like most other verbs in the language.

6.6.2 OLD's

Another useful device to help students understand reverse verbs is OLD's. Suppose a French student says, for example:

†I bore that movie.

Say to him the literal translation of *That movie bores me*:

†Ce film ennui me.

When students have reverse verbs in their own languages, mixing up the *experiencer-stimulus* order will make clear the grammar you are trying to teach them. If they do not have reverse verbs, then using comparisions of straightforward and reverse verbs, as in the preceding scrambling exercise, should make the difference clear.

6.7 Keeping the student's word order

Often the student's intuition in making the stimulus or the experiencer the subject is appropriate. Obviously, when there is only one, either the stimulus or the experiencer, there is no choice.

6.7.1 Using ED form when the experiencer is first

If your students say:

†I surprise!
†He annoys at the mosquitoes.
†We are interesting in sports.

It may be best to stick to their word order *(experiencer-verb-stimulus)* and teach them that the *ED* form of the reverse psychological verb is the only way to maintain that order.

I am surprised!
He is annoyed at the mosquitoes.
We are interested in sports.

6.7.2 Using ING form when the stimulus is first

If students use the wrong verb form with the stimulus first, they will produce goofs like these:

†The game's very excited, isn't it?
†That is not amused at all!

They may just need to learn that if the stimulus appears first, the *ING* form must be used:

> The game's very exciting, isn't it?
> That is not amusing at all!

6.8 Using ING and ED forms in redundant sentences

The use of both forms at once may help reinforce the rules that *ING* modifies the stimulus and *ED* modifies the experiencer. Give the students a few sample sentences using both forms of the same verb:

> I was fascinated by the fascinating movie.
> The children were amused by the amusing monkey .

Then give them reverse verbs and have them devise similar redundant sentences.

Cue:	Satisfy.
Response:	We were satisfied by the satisfying meal.
Cue:	Annoy.
Response:	I am annoyed by annoying people.

With your encouragement, students may develop many such sentences in this form. They should, however, realize that this is a practice technique, and that such redundancy would have a somewhat unnatural or amusing effect in ordinary communication.